Cambridge English Advanced 5

WITH ANSWERS

Authentic examination papers from Cambridge ESOL

CAMBRIDGE
UNIVERSITY PRESS

CAMBRIDGE UNIVERSITY PRESS
Cambridge, New York, Melbourne, Madrid, Cape Town,
Singapore, São Paulo, Delhi, Mexico City

Cambridge University Press
The Edinburgh Building, Cambridge CB2 8RU, UK

www.cambridge.org
Information on this title: www.cambridge.org/9781107603257

First published 2012

Printed in the United Kingdom at the University Press, Cambridge

A catalogue record for this book is available from the British Library

ISBN 978-1-107-603233 Student's Book without answers
ISBN 978-1-107-603257 Student's Book with answers
ISBN 978-1-107-603264 Audio CD Set
ISBN 978-1-107-603271 Self-study Pack

Cambridge University Press has no responsibility for the persistence or
accuracy of URLs for external or third-party internet websites referred to in
this publication, and does not guarantee that any content on such websites is,
or will remain, accurate or appropriate. Information regarding prices, travel
timetables and other factual information given in this work is correct at
the time of first printing but Cambridge University Press does not guarantee
the accuracy of such information thereafter.

Contents

Introduction

This collection of four complete practice tests comprises papers from the *Cambridge English: Advanced*, also known as *Certificate in Advanced English (CAE)*, examination; students can practise these tests on their own or with the help of a teacher.

The *Cambridge English: Advanced* examination is part of a suite of general English examinations produced by Cambridge ESOL. This suite consists of five examinations that have similar characteristics but are designed for different levels of English language ability. Within the five levels, *Cambridge English: Advanced* is at Level C1 in the Council of Europe's *Common European Framework of Reference for Languages: Learning, teaching, assessment*. It has also been accredited in the UK as a Level 2 ESOL certificate in the National Qualifications Framework. The *Cambridge English: Advanced* examination is widely recognised in commerce and industry and in individual university faculties and other educational institutions.

Examination	Council of Europe Framework Level	UK National Qualifications Framework Level
Cambridge English: Proficiency *Certificate of Proficiency in English (CPE)*	C2	3
Cambridge English: Advanced *Certificate in Advanced English (CAE)*	C1	2
Cambridge English: First *First Certificate in English (FCE)*	B2	1
Cambridge English: Preliminary *Preliminary English Test (PET)*	B1	Entry 3
Cambridge English: Key *Key English Test (KET)*	A2	Entry 2

Further information

The information contained in this practice book is designed to be an overview of the exam. For a full description of all of the above exams, including information about task types, testing focus and preparation, please see the relevant handbooks which can be obtained from Cambridge ESOL at the address below or from the website at: www.cambridgeesol.org

University of Cambridge ESOL Examinations
1 Hills Road
Cambridge CB1 2EU
United Kingdom

Telephone: +44 1223 553997
Fax: +44 1223 553621
e-mail: ESOLHelpdesk@ucles.org.uk

The structure of *Cambridge English: Advanced* – an overview

The *Cambridge English: Advanced* examination consists of five papers.

Paper 1   Reading   1 hour 15 minutes
This paper consists of **four** parts, each containing one text or several shorter pieces. There are 34 questions in total, including multiple choice, gapped text and multiple matching.

Paper 2   Writing   1 hour 30 minutes
This paper consists of **two** parts which carry equal marks. In Part 1, which is **compulsory**, input material of up to 150 words is provided on which candidates have to base their answers. Candidates have to write either an article, a letter, a proposal or a report of between 180 and 220 words.
   In Part 2, there are **four** tasks from which candidates **choose one** to write about. The range of tasks from which questions may be drawn includes an article, a competition entry, a contribution to a longer piece, an essay, an information sheet, a letter, a proposal, a report and a review. The last question is based on the set books. These books remain on the list for two years. Look on the website, or contact the Cambridge ESOL Centre Exams Manager in your area for the up-to-date list of set books. The question on the set books has two options from which candidates **choose one** to write about. In this part, candidates have to write between 220 and 260 words.

Paper 3   Use of English   45 minutes
This paper consists of **five** parts and tests control of English grammar and vocabulary. There are 50 questions in total. The tasks include gap-filling exercises, word formation, lexical appropriacy and sentence transformation.

Paper 4   Listening   40 minutes (approximately)
This paper consists of **four** parts. Each part contains a recorded text or texts and some questions including multiple choice, sentence completion and multiple matching. There is a total of 30 questions. Each text is heard twice.

Paper 5   Speaking   15 minutes
This paper consists of **four** parts. The standard test format is two candidates and two examiners. One examiner takes part in the conversation while the other examiner listens. Both examiners give marks. Candidates will be given photographs and other visual and written material to look at and talk about. Sometimes candidates will talk with the other candidates, sometimes with the examiner and sometimes with both.

Grading

The overall *Cambridge English*: *Advanced* grade is based on the total score gained in all five papers. Each paper is weighted to 40 marks. Therefore, the five *Cambridge English*: *Advanced* papers total 200 marks, after weighting. It is not necessary to achieve a satisfactory level in all five papers in order to pass the examination. Certificates are given to candidates who pass the examination with grade A, B or C. A is the highest. Exceptional candidates sometimes show ability beyond C1 level. Candidates who achieve grade A receive the *Cambridge English*: *Advanced* certificate stating that they demonstrated ability at Level C2. Candidates who achieve a grade B or C receive the *Cambridge English*: *Advanced* certificate at Level C1. Candidates whose performance is below C1 level, but falls within Level B2, receive a Cambridge English certificate stating that they have demonstrated ability at B2 level. All candidates are sent a Statement of Results which includes a graphical profile of their performance in each paper and shows their relative performance in each one.

For further information on grading and results, go to the website (see page 4).

Test 1

PAPER 1   READING (1 hour 15 minutes)

Part 1

You are going to read three extracts which are all concerned in some way with science and technology. For questions **1–6**, choose the answer (**A**, **B**, **C** or **D**) which you think fits best according to the text.

Mark your answers **on the separate answer sheet**.

Introducing 'de-perimeterisation'

It is an ugly word, but 'de-perimeterisation' should be jangling the nerves of the business world in ways that have nothing to do with its discordant phonetics. Essentially it spells the end of the world as we have known it. The harbingers of this particular digital doom are email, the Internet, laptop computers, mobile phones, Blackberries and any other way in which information, both innocuous and malicious, can enter or leave an organisation unhindered by such traditional electronic defences as the firewall and the scanners for viruses and spam.

The Jericho Forum, set up a few years ago, is an international lobby that includes some of the big multi-nationals. It emphasises the need for a proactive approach, warning: 'Over the next few years, as technology and business continue to align more closely to an open, internet-driven world, the current security mechanisms that protect business information will not match the increasing demands for protection of business transactions and data.'

line 2

line 5

line 12
line 13

1   Which word in the text is used to stress the vulnerability of information stored on companies' computer systems?

   A   jangling (line 2)
   B   discordant (line 5)
   C   innocuous (line 12)
   D   unhindered (line 13)

2   According to the text, what type of action does the Jericho Forum propose?

   A   working together to deal with the effects of a problem
   B   looking at how to cut down the volume of sensitive business data
   C   looking ahead to deal with the predicted effects of certain developments
   D   working to ensure that electronic means of communication are used effectively

What is Design?

The volume of stuff that seems to warrant inclusion in the category that we might call 'design' has increased enormously in recent years, as has the number of people who create, manufacture, retail and consume it – not to mention those employed to critique or champion it in the media. But our understanding of design is outdated, limited by definitions from the beginning of the last century, when concepts such as consumerism, lifestyle, popular culture and marketing were in their infancy. The landscape has changed and new maps are required to make sense of it.

A recent row at London's Design Museum is a symptom of the mismatch between ideology and reality. Chairman James Dyson – a maverick designer-engineer who made his fortune with his 'cyclonic' vacuum cleaner – resigned over the museum's change in direction under director Alice Rawsthorn, who, he believes, has betrayed the museum's founding mission to 'encourage serious design of the manufactured object'.

Dyson's website defines design as 'how something works, not how it looks – the design should evolve from the function'. His vacuum cleaners are ostensibly pure expressions of the mechanics of dust sucking. According to Dyson, Rawsthorn's exhibition programme presents design as 'shallow style'. He claims it pursues a populist agenda at the expense of one that encourages an appreciation of the processes leading to manufactured objects which perform better than their predecessors. Rawsthorn, reluctant to reignite the row, would not give us a definition, but did say she was seeking 'a modern definition of diverse and inclusive design'.

3   In this extract, the writer is

    A   questioning the relevance of one man's definition of the word 'design'.
    B   complaining about the imprecise way the word 'design' is now used.
    C   lending his support to one interpretation of the meaning of 'design'.
    D   calling for a re-evaluation of what is meant by the word 'design'.

4   From the extract, we learn that Alice Rawsthorn does not

    A   want to prolong her argument with James Dyson.
    B   mind what James Dyson says about her work at the museum.
    C   agree that the museum was set up to promote one type of design.
    D   accept that she has altered the focus of the museum's exhibitions.

Interview with Dr Andrew Steele, Astrobiologist

Steele: If I said that I'd sat down and planned any of this, I'd be lying through my teeth. I just took advantage of opportunities as they came up. In 1996, news broke that this bloke from NASA thought he'd found life on Mars. I was just coming to the end of my PhD studentship and I'd done some high-powered imaging of bacteria, and this scientist from NASA had got images of what he thought were bacteria on the surface of a meteorite. So, I phoned international directory enquiries and got his number, phoned him up and said: 'I can get you better images than that.' And to cut a long story short, he sent me a bit of meteorite. People imagine it took guts to ring up, but it didn't really. In Houston, they asked: 'Who's speaking?' And I said: 'Dr Steele.' I'd had my PhD all of three weeks at that point.

So, me and a couple of mates ended up in my room trying to figure out what to do, with a piece of Mars sat in the middle of the table. My friends said: 'Steele, what've you done?' I said: 'I don't know. I told him I could get better images.' So we planned it out and did some good research, and then NASA offered me a job. I'd always been interested in biology, but never knew what to do with it. I did the PhD to give myself options, to open doors. I sort of object to systems that pigeonhole you early on. That's a load of rubbish.

5   In the first paragraph, Dr Steele is

   A   describing how he put his career plans into practice.
   B   explaining how he first got involved in a project.
   C   showing how easily he fooled a famous scientist.
   D   relating the story of a very risky thing that he did.

6   In describing his experiences, Dr Steele reveals his

   A   nostalgia for his student days.
   B   pride in his academic qualifications.
   C   confidence in his abilities.
   D   dismissive attitude towards his colleagues.

Part 2

You are going to read an extract from a magazine article. Six paragraphs have been removed from the extract. Choose from the paragraphs **A–G** the one which fits each gap (**7–12**). There is one extra paragraph which you do not need to use.
Mark your answers **on the separate answer sheet**.

Spadework that's truly rewarding

Tony Durrant volunteers on an archaeological dig

As I squatted in the mud, on what looked like a building site, to scrape at the ground with a tiny trowel, I wondered if fictional archaeologists like Indiana Jones started their careers in such damp circumstances. Probably not. But it is what real archaeologists do, and I was surrounded by them as they burrowed their way into centuries of Canterbury's hidden past.

7	

The muddy land that I found myself on, I hoped, would soon reveal its historical treasures. About 60 metres square and catchily titled the 'Big Dig', it is one of the largest and most exciting projects of its type in Britain. The Canterbury Archaeological Trust is responsible for the unearthing of this small area of a city filled with echoes of the past.

8	

There are many tonnes of earth to shift and sift and hundreds of finds to clean and sort, which is why volunteers are here. Surprisingly, they are given as much responsibility as many of the paid archaeologists. This level of faith in unpaid help can work only if the volunteers are committed to a regular slot or come for a few days at a time.

9	

Sarah Turner, a law student in term time, is spending her short break scratching around at the bottom of a medieval rubbish pit. So far, she has pulled out clay pipes and early glassware. 'This sort of archaeology isn't about the rare finds – it is about the many mundane things that allow us to build a big historical picture,' says Sarah. She also includes a word of warning about the physical nature of the job.

10	

As if on cue, the cold drizzle started again and surprisingly elicited little reaction from the crouched figures beavering away – a testament to their professionalism. I returned to my scraping and watched for any differently coloured patches of soil – a sign of ancient earth floors, buried foundations and ditches.

11	

The lost or discarded minutiae of life in this once-crowded little area are being painstakingly uncovered: cooked animal bones, the occasional coin. Everything of possible interest is taken to the 'finds office', where more volunteers, under the watchful eye of Jacqui Lawrence, wash, document and bag them. Jacqui, a trust employee, has a lot of time for volunteers; she started off as one herself.

12	

'I love Roman pottery. Look at this. What a beautifully made piece,' she says, handing me what looked like the base of a jug. Then she passed over a piece of Roman roof tile. Touching the past, feeling the excitement of handling something for the first time since it was discarded all those years ago – this is what archaeology is all about!

A 'This allows us, after an initial period of training, to get more involved in the project,' says one. 'We can then get a lot more fulfilment out of our time here than if we popped in once to be given some dull task.'

B 'Volunteers, including myself, are often surprised at how rough and ready it is,' she adds. 'They expect to be scraping around with a toothbrush. But the only way we can get all this earth shifted is with a large spade, and we are well behind schedule because of unpredictable conditions.'

C On the contrary, there in front of me was the most exciting find yet! Twelve tiny statues buried in the damp clay along the far wall of the church. I watched a young woman archaeologist carefully tending to one. They would all be meticulously recorded before heading for the museum.

D This preparatory 'housework' was essential before the medieval layer we were standing on could be stripped away. This would allow the archaeologists to make sense of the jumble around them: a 19th-century bottle dump, a medieval rubbish pit and a Roman floor lay within metres of each other.

E Dressed like them in white hard hat and luminous green vest, I clambered in and out of trenches and pits, sketching, photographing and shovelling. Since my life had lacked much of an exercise routine, joining an archaeological project near the centre of the city seemed ideal.

F Its main aim had already been achieved: the uncovering of part of a church built in 1318. Now, the diggers have all but stripped away this layer of history, to search for evidence of life in early medieval, Anglo-Saxon, Roman, and they hope, Iron-Age Canterbury.

G 'I always wanted to be a career archaeologist,' she says, carefully writing an identification code on a piece of pottery under the watchful eyes of the team's pin-up: who else but the actor Harrison Ford, in character as the great Indiana Jones.

Part 3

You are going to read an article from a music magazine. For questions **13–19**, choose the answer
(**A**, **B**, **C** or **D**) which you think fits best according to the text.
Mark your answers **on the separate answer sheet**.

Never too old to rock

Clive Myrtle explores the issue of ageism in the world of entertainment

There are few spectacles less edifying than a television presenter trying to hang on to a job. When
one of the presenters of the BBC programme *Crimewatch* resigned recently, rather than suffer the
inevitable indignity of being uninstalled and replaced by a younger version, he made the usual hurt
noises about his masters' excessive emphasis on youth. People in the media listened sympathetically
before he slid from view with a soft splosh to join the ranks of television's has-beens.

The presenter's argument, that the viewers don't care how old you are so long as you can 'do the
job', unfortunately is not backed up by the evidence. When you're on TV, viewers are always thinking
about whether you're losing your hair or your figure and, latterly, whether you've had cosmetic work
done. This is what they're actually doing when you think they're listening to the wise things you say.
Viewers actually don't perceive much of what the job entails, they just see you sitting there looking
the part. Like double-jointedness or the ability to pat one's head while rubbing one's stomach, TV
presenting is just one of those knacks. Some of those who possess this knack can hit the big time.
Inevitably as they become more attached to the lifestyle this brings, however, the more inclined they
are to overstate the knack.

In reality, if somebody is paying you a lot of money to do a job, it's often on the tacit understanding
that your services may be dispensed with abruptly – it's part of the deal. Unlike football managers,
TV presenters affect not to understand this brutal compact. If they've had many years being paid silly
sums to read a script from an autocue, it's difficult for them to accept that they've been the beneficiary
of good fortune rather than anything else; even harder to face the fact that a commissioning editor's
whim could all too easily banish them to the shopping channels.

Something similar eventually awaits all the people who are currently making fortunes that would
have been unimaginable to earlier generations of presenters. One day we'll decide that their face no
longer fits and they'll be dragged away complaining about the same ageist policy from which they no
doubt previously profited. Show business is a brutal business. The one thing it reliably punishes is
age, particularly amongst women. That's why, at the age of fifty, female TV presenters become female
radio presenters and why girl bands planning to re-form need to get it done before they're forty, after
which it will get too hard for everyone to suspend their collective disbelief.

Only one species of show-business folk manages to hold back the years and this is a group that, by
rights, shouldn't. Its members should, like all childish things, have been put away years ago. And yet
they keep on performing as if there was no tomorrow. I'm talking about rock stars, usually male ones.
As these heroes of a bygone era drift into the pensionable zone, they may no longer sell records in the
way that they used to, but they have a power to magnetise huge sections of the population – and part
them from their cash – that makes them the envy of everybody else in the show-business fraternity.

The likes of Bruce Springsteen, Mick Jagger and Elton John sailed past their fiftieth and sixtieth
birthdays with barely a mumble of complaint from their fans. The larger the scale of their sold-out
shows, the more distant they are from audiences and the less noticeable are their jowls or their
waistlines. People wonder why the stadiums are dominated by acts who made their names thirty
years ago; is it indicative of some fatal streak of nostalgia running through the music business?
Hardly. It simply proves that in this day and age, the Hot New Thing can never be quite as hot as the
Hot Old Thing. Rock musicians may not have had the fat monthly salaries enjoyed by their grumbling
autocue-reading counterparts on TV, but they have something their parents would never have
predicted when they quit school and first joined a band – a job for life.

line 13 (beside paragraph 2, final lines)

line 38 (beside final paragraph)

13 What does the writer imply about the *Crimewatch* presenter he mentions in the first paragraph?

    A   He was unwise to resign when he did.
    B   He will soon be forgotten by the viewers.
    C   He may well have had a valid point to make.
    D   He was treated insensitively by his employers.

14 The word 'this' in line 13 refers to

    A   an image.
    B   a level of success.
    C   an exaggerated claim.
    D   a common misperception.

15 Why does the writer mention football managers in the third paragraph?

    A   to show how relatively secure TV presenters are in their jobs
    B   to underline how important luck is in certain occupations
    C   to illustrate a general rule about certain types of high-profile jobs
    D   to support his view that presenters are overpaid

16 In the fourth paragraph, the writer says that TV personalities who may worry about ageism

    A   should look for work in other forms of broadcasting.
    B   may have benefited from it themselves at some point.
    C   are less well respected than the presenters of the past.
    D   are being unfair to up-and-coming younger colleagues.

17 The word 'it' in line 38 refers to

    A   the size of the venues played by ageing rock stars.
    B   the way ageing rock stars keep their fans at a distance.
    C   the backward-looking nature of the rock music business.
    D   the continuing appeal of live performances by certain stars.

18 Why does the writer mention rock stars' parents in the final paragraph?

    A   to underline an irony about the stars' careers
    B   to remind us of the stars' humble beginnings
    C   to put the stars' ongoing popularity in context
    D   to expose an inconsistency in the stars' attitude

19 In the text as a whole, the writer reveals himself to be

    A   critical of show-business personalities who complain.
    B   concerned about the way certain celebrities are treated.
    C   supportive of older people in the world of entertainment.
    D   envious of the success of certain high-profile performers.

Part 4

You are going to read an article in which five specialists talk about the value of drawing. For questions **20–34**, choose from the sections of the article (**A–E**). The sections may be chosen more than once.

Note: When more than one answer is required, these may be given **in any order**.

Mark your answers **on the separate answer sheet**.

Which specialist(s)

suggests it's possible to be discouraged by the degree of detail a subject presents?	20
says that, as a result of the drawing process, you may notice details you were previously unaware of?	21
produces work which hasn't been adapted from previous attempts?	22
mentions how different materials can directly affect the production of a drawing?	23
states that drawing is a means of both gaining knowledge and expressing oneself?	24
consider that drawing involves the artist's ability to choose what is important?	25 26
say a technically good drawing, produced without emotion, will remain unconvincing?	27 28
states that the ability to draw can help the artist to have confidence in their own ideas?	29
believes that technology has created an even greater need for drawing by hand?	30
mentions the need to work whenever the desire to draw occurs?	31
mentions how realistic and creative approaches to drawing can be combined?	32
comments that the majority of people do not go on to increase their potential for drawing?	33
mentions that, in the process of producing a finished picture, a preliminary sketch will grow in significance?	34

An Undying Art

We asked five specialists what drawing can teach us, how they use it and how they see its future in the computer age

A   Laura Gascoigne – Art critic

It is in drawing that you can test the truth of an artist's statement, whether a picture is telling you what he or she feels. A slick drawing, made for its own sake rather than as an expression of a genuine response, will have an air of falsity about it, no matter how you dress it up. Although looking lies at the heart of all drawing practice, developing this ability is only one reason for drawing. As a form of communication, drawing is just as valid as writing. But whereas we continue to develop our writing skills and exploit them fully in our adult lives, our drawing skills are often stuck at a childish stage of development we are ashamed of.

B   Quentin Blake – Children's artist

Drawing is a way of informing yourself, just as it's a way of explaining yourself to others. When you stand in front of something to draw it, you're presented with an overwhelming amount of information which you can find dismaying. When I do roughs for illustrations, I'm using experience and instinct to discover how the subjects are reacting; I may put them in a posture I hadn't thought about but merely felt. There's a particular co-ordination between hand and eye that makes one person's work distinctively their own. Drawing may be threatened in some way by computers, but even if people have to work on a screen, they'll still have a fundamental need to draw.

C   Deanna Petherbridge – Professor of drawing

The ability to draw teaches people how to look. Drawing's about looking and therefore discovering your artistic originality in what you create, because we all look with our eyes and see quite differently. It gives one a sense of self in the world. It leads one to trust one's judgement and trains us to select what's significant. In my work, I've never done preliminary drawing, because it's difficult to repeat something or continue when the urgency's gone. I work in drawing as a final product. It's my entire visual art practice; I eat, sleep, think, write about and do drawing. Drawing is absolutely essential to a technological age. Now that people are constantly working on the computer, the ability to invent things rather than just use existing images is more essential than ever, and it can only come through drawing.

D   Anthony Eyton – Painter

Drawing is a very good exercise because you have to put your hand where your brain is. When you draw a landscape you realise it's much more complicated than you thought. You suddenly see rhythms and spaces you hadn't taken in. In a restaurant or gallery I'll suddenly see something with fresh eyes, and that's the moment I pounce and reach for my pencil and paper and get very annoyed if I don't have any. This is the 'wandering-about-in-the-street' sort of drawing, when your fingers get itchy and you get the message. When I go on to produce a painting from it, I may start in a random way thinking about colour, but the drawing will become more important, as a point of reference; this sort of drawing is about getting things in the right place. There's room for technology and there's room for drawing. Drawing will always be needed to express our thoughts and ideas. Clever drawing can sometimes be so polished that you can see it doesn't come from the heart; that's the dangerous side of drawing. I'd rather think of it as a personal thing you have to do.

E   Peter Randall-Page – Sculptor

There's objective drawing and there's drawing from an idea in your imagination – and a sliding scale between the two. To a large extent, drawing is a process of editing, of deciding what is an essential quality. I always carry a sketchbook, but I also use drawing to explain things to clients or engineers. Then there's 'thinking' drawing – when I'm grappling with an idea in my mind and I bring it to the surface; I use this together with preliminary models when I'm developing ideas for sculptures. I also do a lot of drawings for simple pleasure. I don't feel drawing is threatened by computers. In a sense, you're always limited by your tools; your imagination might be bound by what a computer can actually do. Similarly, the act of drawing is determined by friction, the difference between a ballpoint sliding all over the place and charcoal crunching across the surface of heavy paper. The computer doesn't offer anything I can't do better without one.

PAPER 2 WRITING (1 hour 30 minutes)

Part 1

You **must** answer this question. Write your answer in **180–220** words in an appropriate style.

---

1 You have been a student at an international college in Ireland for the past month. The student committee has asked you to write a report about your first week in the college.

Read the Programme of Events for New Students, and the extracts from your diary below. Then, **using the information appropriately**, write a report to inform the committee, saying what was helpful about the events, explaining any problems you had and suggesting any changes for the future.

Programme of Events for New Students

Monday	College tour
Tuesday	Meeting with tutors
Wednesday	Talks about clubs
Thursday	Tour of town
Friday	Social evening

Monday	Useful tour but I'll never remember it all. Need a map!
Tuesday	Excellent info about course. Staff helpful.
Wednesday	Joined basketball club. Made some friends too!
Thursday	Exhausted – too much walking!
Friday	Great party. Finished too early...

Write your **report**. You should use your own words as far as possible.

Part 2

Write an answer to **one** of the questions **2–5** in this part. Write your answer in **220–260** words in an appropriate style.

---

2 Your teacher has asked you to write an essay on the following subject:

Our leisure activities and hobbies have been changed dramatically by technology. To what extent do you agree with this?

Write your **essay**.

3 You see this announcement in a magazine.

> **AN OPPORTUNITY TO TRAVEL AND HELP CHILDREN**
>
> We organise education projects in various countries and are looking for volunteers to teach children how to read and write in English. We will provide any necessary training.
>
> To apply, write giving details of any experience or qualifications you have which may be relevant and saying why you would like to work with children.
>
> Anna Graham, Manager, Eduprojects Worldwide

Write your **letter of application**.

4 You see the following announcement in an international film magazine.

> Have you ever wanted to be Spiderman or Lara Croft? Imagine you could live the life of any film character for one day. We would like our readers to write an article telling us:
>
> • which character from a film you would like to be
> • why you would like to be this character
> • what your day as your character would be like.

Write your **article**.

5 Answer **one** of the following two questions based on **one** of the titles below.

(a) *Through a Glass, Darkly* by Donna Leon

You have had a class discussion about the plot of *Through a Glass, Darkly*. Now your teacher has asked you to write an essay on the following topic:

Through a Glass, Darkly *is a sequence of thrilling events with a surprising ending. To what extent do you agree with this?*

Write your **essay**.

(b) *Of Mice and Men* by John Steinbeck

Your college magazine has asked you to write an article on a memorable event that takes place in *Of Mice and Men*. Describe an event, explain why you think it is memorable and say why it is important to the story.

Write your **article**.

PAPER 3   USE OF ENGLISH (1 hour)

Part 1

For questions **1–12**, read the text below and decide which answer (**A**, **B**, **C** or **D**) best fits each gap. There is an example at the beginning (**0**).

Mark your answers **on the separate answer sheet**.

Example:

0 A necessity   **B** reliance   **C** demand   **D** requirement

0	A	B	C	D
	☐	▬	☐	☐

Early map-making

Satellite navigation in cars means that our traditional **(0)** .... on printed maps and road atlases for finding our way to a destination is disappearing. Yet as **(1)** .... of beauty to look at for both pleasure and serious research, maps, ancient and modern, still **(2)** .... strongly to our imaginations as they are the result of amazingly **(3)** .... observation of the real world. After the invention of the printing press in the fifteenth century, maps could be reproduced in greater numbers, and as mathematics and technology transformed surveying and navigation, their accuracy **(4)** .... improved.

Today, it is the inaccuracies in these early maps that we find so fascinating. The map-maker would fill in the huge gaps in his knowledge with guesswork. Dull **(5)** .... of ocean, for example, would be **(6)** .... with drawings of fantastic sea creatures or plump babies with puffed-out cheeks blowing along ships in full **(7)** ....

The world's first modern atlas **(8)** .... in Antwerp in 1570, after a geographer named Abraham Ortelius **(9)** .... engravings of 53 of the best maps **(10)** .... at that time and organised them in a logical sequence in a book. This atlas reflected the **(11)** .... of contemporary knowledge by showing Australia as an uncharted southern continent labelled 'not yet known southern land'. Over the next 40 years, this atlas was regularly **(12)** .... and more than 7,300 copies were printed.

1   **A** cases   **B** articles   **C** objects   **D** pieces

2   **A** appeal   **B** engage   **C** interest   **D** attract

3   **A** complex   **B** involved   **C** elaborate   **D** detailed

4   **A** smoothly   **B** evenly   **C** steadily   **D** equally

5   **A** spreads   **B** breadths   **C** ranges   **D** expanses

6   **A** revived   **B** enlivened   **C** invigorated   **D** enlightened

7   **A** force   **B** length   **C** flow   **D** sail

8   **A** exhibited   **B** presented   **C** appeared   **D** arose

9   **A** appointed   **B** commissioned   **C** engaged   **D** assigned

10 **A** in existence   **B** at large   **C** in stock   **D** at present

11 **A** edges   **B** borders   **C** limits   **D** verges

12 **A** renovated   **B** updated   **C** modernised   **D** renewed

Part 2

For questions **13–27**, read the text below and think of the word which best fits each gap. Use only **one** word in each gap. There is an example at the beginning (**0**).

Write your answers **IN CAPITAL LETTERS on the separate answer sheet**.

Example:

0	L	I	K	E														

The game of 'Go'

Liao Xingwen, **(0)** .... most six-year-old boys, enjoys playing games. What is unusual is that **(13)** .... one Liao plays happens to **(14)** .... one of the most challenging board games in the world. Liao, who lives in the Chinese city of Guilin, is learning to master 'Go', which was invented over 4,000 years ago by Chinese emperors and used **(15)** .... an aid in working out military strategy. Around fifty million people in East Asia play 'Go', some of **(16)** .... high-earning professionals. One indication **(17)** .... the game's popularity is the high number of viewers that televised matches attract in Japan and China. Ever **(18)** .... he was five, Liao has lived apart **(19)** .... his parents. He's looked after by a couple of professional players, under **(20)** .... guidance he plays for anything **(21)** .... to eight hours a day.

(22) .... the rules of 'Go' are fairly simple, the technique needed is fiendishly difficult. It is claimed that the game takes two minutes to learn but **(23)** .... lifetime to master. The board on **(24)** .... 'Go' is played consists of a series of vertical and horizontal lines, and players mark out territory on it with their stones and try to capture their opponent's stones.

Professionals are ranked **(25)** .... a scale from one to nine and Liao's ambition is to become a level nine player one day. Liao is now taking part in a Mind Sports competition in London **(26)** .... as many as forty challenging mind sports are being played. **(27)** .... so, 'Go' is still considered the most difficult game in the competition.

Part 3

For questions **28–37**, read the text below. Use the word given in capitals at the end of some of the lines to form a word that fits in the gap **in the same line**. There is an example at the beginning (**0**).

Write your answers **IN CAPITAL LETTERS on the separate answer sheet**.

Example: | 0 | G | E | N | E | R | A | L | L | Y | | | | | | | | |

The Victoria Falls

The Victoria Falls in Africa are neither the highest nor the widest
waterfall in the world, but they are (**0**) …….. regarded as the largest. The   **GENERAL**
(**28**) …….. for this view is that their width of 1.7 kilometres and height of 108   **BASE**
metres form the largest sheet of (**29**) …….. water in the world. Furthermore,   **CASCADE**
the Victoria Falls come out well if a (**30**) …….. is made between their flow   **COMPARE**
rate and that of other falls.

For a (**31**) …….. distance above the falls, the Zambezi River flows over a   **CONSIDER**
level sheet of basalt. Dotted along its course are tree-covered islands which
become more (**32**) …….. as the river approaches the falls.   **NUMBER**

The falls are formed as the river drops into a chasm 60–120 metres wide. The
(**33**) …….. of the chasm ranges between 80 and 108 metres. There are two   **DEEP**
islands on the crest of the falls that separate the curtain of water into parallel
streams. When there is a reduction in water flow, (**34**) …….. islands appear.   **ADD**

The unusual form of the Victoria Falls (**35**) …….. virtually the whole width of   **ABLE**
the falls to be viewed face-on from as close as 60 metres. (**36**) …….. few   **RELATE**
waterfalls allow such a close approach on foot, which partly explains why
the falls are becoming (**37**) …….. popular as a tourist destination.   **INCREASE**

Part 4

For questions **38–42**, think of **one** word only which can be used appropriately in all three sentences. Here is an example (**0**).

Example:

0 They say the new minister is a lovely person and very ……………….. to talk to.

   My neighbours have not had a very ……………….. life, but they always seem cheerful.

   It's ……………….. enough to see why the town is popular with tourists.

Example:	**0**	E	A	S	Y													

Write **only** the missing word **IN CAPITAL LETTERS on the separate answer sheet.**

---

38 I'm sorry I'm so late – the traffic was particularly ……………….. because of the road works.

   Whenever you pick up something like a ……………….. box, it is important to bend both legs in order to protect your back.

   The new job brought with it long hours and ……………….. responsibilities.

39 No matter how often the house was cleaned, during the dry season everything seemed to be permanently covered with a fine ……………….. of dust.

   Hardly anyone seems to buy ……………….. for their cameras these days because most people use digital ones.

   Several reviewers think that this ……………….. will become one of the great classics of our time.

40 The strikers are demanding better ……………….. conditions and more pay.

   I don't know a huge amount about computers but I have a good ……………….. knowledge.

   The best thing in the transport museum was a ……………….. model of a steam engine, which was perfect in every detail.

41 My sister ……………….. the money she needed for her trip to Australia by selling her stamp collection.

The new measures announced by the Government will ensure that low standards in schools will soon be ……………….. as promised.

The bridge is ……………….. several times a day to allow ships to sail up the river.

42 I asked Keith the shortest way to the station and he ……………….. me a map on the back of an envelope.

The authors of the report ……………….. a number of conclusions from their research, which I will try to summarise in a moment.

Last time they played ice hockey, Canada ……………….. against Russia and it'll be interesting to see what happens this time.

Part 5

For questions **43–50**, complete the second sentence so that it has a similar meaning to the first sentence, using the word given. **Do not change the word given.** You must use between **three** and **six** words, including the word given. Here is an example (**0**).

Example:

0 James would only speak to the head of department alone.

   ON

   James ………………………………… to the head of department alone.

The gap can be filled with the words 'insisted on speaking', so you write:

Example: | **0** | INSISTED ON SPEAKING

Write **only** the missing words **IN CAPITAL LETTERS**.

---

43 Lucy succeeded in passing her driving test, even though she had flu.

   MANAGED

   Despite ………………………………… her driving test.

44 By the end of the meeting, the committee had agreed on the next step.

   REACHED

   By the end of the committee meeting, an ………………………………… what to do next.

45 The burglar wore gloves so as not to leave any fingerprints behind.

   AVOID

   The burglar wore gloves in ………………………………… any fingerprints behind.

46 Colin couldn't possibly afford any of the paintings in that gallery.

   FAR

   The paintings in that gallery are ………………………………… buy.

47   I was very shocked when my brother told me what had happened the previous day.

ACCOUNT

I was very shocked by my .... what had happened the previous day.

48   I don't think we'll see Simon before he goes to New York.

LIKELIHOOD

There's .... Simon before he goes to New York.

49   The fire at the oil depot has led to the imposition of stricter safety regulations.

IMPOSED

Stricter safety regulations .... result of the fire at the oil depot.

50   If you hadn't helped me, I could never have moved the wardrobe.

HELP

But .... , I could never have moved the wardrobe.

PAPER 4   LISTENING (approximately 40 minutes)

Part 1

You will hear three different extracts. For questions **1–6**, choose the answer (**A**, **B** or **C**) which fits best according to what you hear. There are two questions for each extract.

Extract One

You overhear two friends talking about holidays.

1   How is the man feeling at present?

   A   pleased with himself

   B   ready for a rest

   C   keen to move house

2   The woman is encouraging her friend to

   A   spend a lot of money.

   B   travel all around Europe.

   C   support ethical tourism.

Extract Two

You hear part of an interview with a woman called Jane Hilton, who takes part in the sport of free climbing.

3   Why does Jane compare free climbing to chess?

   A   Both call for a regular commitment of time.

   B   Both require you to think ahead.

   C   Both involve taking chances.

4   What motivates Jane to do free climbing?

   A   It allows her flexibility in her lifestyle.

   B   She can take responsibility for her own decisions.

   C   It evokes an emotional response in her.

Extract Three

You overhear part of a conversation about diving in underwater forests of kelp, which is a type of marine plant.

5   The woman mentions birds in order to emphasise the way divers in kelp forests

    A   feel physically involved in the marine environment.

    B   can appreciate the beauty of the light.

    C   make use of their own natural skills.

6   The man and woman agree that diving in kelp may be difficult because divers

    A   sometimes use their equipment wrongly.

    B   are unable to find their way through.

    C   cannot swim side by side.

Part 2

You will hear a man called Kevin Riley talking about his unusual home in Australia. For questions **7–14**, complete the sentences.

An unusual home

Kevin found his job as a successful [_____ **7**] very stressful.

Many traditional Australian buildings are designed to avoid putting

[_____ **8**] on the earth.

Kevin had a total of [_____ **9**] removed before he built his new home.

Kevin produces [_____ **10**] in a hut near his home.

Most of the wood in Kevin's home is now a [_____ **11**] colour.

The materials used to make Kevin's chair were

[_____ **12**] and driftwood.

Kevin remembers that a lack of

[_____ **13**] plus a rich diet used to make him feel sleepy.

Kevin compares the process of constructing his home to a [_____ **14**]

Part 3

You will hear an interview with a man called Seth Jeavons, who organises an annual three-day pop-music festival. For questions **15–20**, choose the answer (**A**, **B**, **C** or **D**) which fits best according to what you hear.

15 According to Seth, what mistake do people who are going to camp at the festival frequently make?

   A They forget how cold it can be at night.
   B They take nothing to sleep on.
   C They have no form of light.
   D They underestimate the size of tent needed.

16 Which problem at the festival has now been solved?

   A the space provided for people watching the main band
   B the capacity of the sound system
   C the location of the car parks
   D the level of security for bands

17 Seth believes his festival is more suitable for children than other similar festivals because

   A there are special family cafés with healthy food.
   B specific entertainment is organised for them.
   C there is a separate campsite for families.
   D trained staff are available to look after them.

18 Seth predicts that the bands attracting most people this year will be those which

   A encourage audience participation.
   B have the best special effects.
   C are rarely seen at live events.
   D have the most famous names.

19 According to Seth, why should people go to a big live festival?

   A It will leave a lasting impression on them.
   B The audiences are as interesting as the events.
   C They will see acts not covered by the media.
   D It will be a chance to discover new music.

20 What is Seth reluctant to reveal about next year's festival?

   A the overall scale of the event
   B his daughter's level of involvement
   C the identity of the main band
   D his plans to increase ticket prices

Part 4

You will hear five short extracts in which people are talking about photography courses they have taken.

TASK ONE

For questions **21–25**, choose from the list (**A–H**) each speaker's occupation.

TASK TWO

For questions **26–30**, choose from the list (**A–H**) what each speaker appreciated most about their photography course.

While you listen you must complete both tasks.

A mechanical engineer	**A** the tutor's feedback
B teacher	**B** good value for money
C sculptor	**C** its creative atmosphere
D architect	**D** its wide-ranging content
E website designer	**E** its traditional approach
F journalist	**F** helpful comments from students
G lawyer	**G** the quality of the materials supplied
H driver	**H** its challenging assignments

Speaker 1	21		Speaker 1	26
Speaker 2	22		Speaker 2	27
Speaker 3	23		Speaker 3	28
Speaker 4	24		Speaker 4	29
Speaker 5	25		Speaker 5	30

PAPER 5   SPEAKING (15 minutes)

There are two examiners. One (the interlocutor) conducts the test, providing you with the necessary materials and explaining what you have to do. The other examiner (the assessor) is introduced to you, but then takes no further part in the interaction.

Part 1 (3 minutes)

The interlocutor first asks you and your partner a few questions. The interlocutor asks candidates for some information about themselves, then widens the scope of the questions by asking about e.g. candidates' leisure activities, studies, travel and daily life. Candidates are expected to respond to the interlocutor's questions and listen to what their partner has to say.

Part 2 (a one-minute 'long turn' for each candidate, plus a 30-second response from the second candidate)

You are each given the opportunity to talk for about a minute, and to comment briefly after your partner has spoken.

The interlocutor gives you a set of pictures and asks you to talk about them for about one minute. It is important to listen carefully to the interlocutor's instructions. The interlocutor then asks your partner a question about your pictures and your partner responds briefly.

You are then given another set of pictures to look at. Your partner talks about these pictures for about one minute. This time the interlocutor asks you a question about your partner's pictures and you respond briefly.

Part 3 (approximately 4 minutes)

In this part of the test, you and your partner are asked to talk together. The interlocutor places a new set of pictures on the table between you. This stimulus provides the basis for a discussion. The interlocutor explains what you have to do.

Part 4 (approximately 4 minutes)

The interlocutor asks some further questions, which leads to a more general discussion of what you have talked about in Part 3. You may comment on your partner's answers if you wish.

Test 2

PAPER 1 READING (1 hour 15 minutes)

Part 1

You are going to read three extracts which are all concerned in some way with feelings. For questions **1–6**, choose the answer (**A**, **B**, **C** or **D**) which you think fits best according to the text. Mark your answers **on the separate answer sheet**.

Minds over Matters

One of the main things groups do is generate ideas and opinions and use these to make decisions. It is generally believed that two – or more – heads are better than one when it comes to these aspects of human behaviour. That's why the modern trend in teaching is for students to work in small groups to prepare presentations and why brainstorming is popular in the work context.

It is a carefully selected team, however, not a randomly generated group that makes creative decisions. Such is the view of management guru Meredith Belbin, whose theories on team-building have proved successful in business. 'My favourite number for a team is four, followed by six,' he says. 'Odd numbers don't work – it is better if people operate in complementary pairs. Big committees don't get anything done.'

But surprisingly, research has shown that brainstorming by groups isn't that effective in either the number or quality of ideas generated – that you get better results if you set people to work individually on a problem. Indeed, groups can get things badly wrong, because their thought processes can go awry if they are isolated from external argument and criticism – a process psychologists call 'groupthink' – whereby the group becomes more important than the individuals and comes to believe it can do no wrong.

1   Meredith Belbin feels that the effectiveness of group decisions is related to

   A   the creativity of individual group members.
   B   the attitude of those making up the group.
   C   the skill of those who decide on the group's composition.
   D   the extent to which external factors affect the group's judgement.

2   In the text as a whole, the writer is

   A   justifying certain educational practices.
   B   arguing for more research to take place.
   C   questioning a widely-held assumption.
   D   explaining a contradiction in human behaviour.

Food for thought

Influential chef and entrepreneur Michel Roux arrived in Britain 35 years ago from France, and 'went on a mission to make London a better place for food.' His ethic of excellence is well known. Right now, though, he has a troubled air about him. 'There is no country where more cookery books are bought than the UK, but many people still care more about the petrol they put in their cars than the fuel they put in their bodies. Also, there is a lot of uninformed babbling about food from high and mighty chefs who really know little about it. And if you ask a lot of young people why they want to come into the catering trade, it is because they want to make a fortune by the time they are 25 and then take a back seat.'

Michel fears his vision, in changing the face of British cuisine, is being hijacked by the media celebrity chefs he helped, indirectly, to create. Not that he has any objections to chefs writing books. His own have sold more than a million copies worldwide. It is the overkill that worries him. Nor, he insists, has he anything against chefs on TV in themselves – after all, he was an early pioneer of the cookery programme. 'Don't think I am putting down everyone who cooks on TV,' he says. 'But you have to work hard to understand your subject. If you move too fast, with no work and no feeling, you get nowhere. Everything is happening too quickly. Food is not all about media hype.'

3   What is part of Michel's annoyance about the British food industry?

    A   the controversial views portrayed in books
    B   certain people's resistance to his ideas
    C   the indifference of young consumers
    D   the ignorance of so-called specialists

4   What impression do we get of Michel from the text?

    A   He regrets many of the things he has done.
    B   He is keen not to appear hypocritical.
    C   He is never satisfied with what he achieves.
    D   He is rather stuck in his ways.

The Feelgood Factor

The scientific endeavour to understand the hows and whys of 'human happiness' has generated in excess of three thousand studies since the 1960s. As a result, psychologists now tend to agree that happier people are more popular and lead much longer and more productive lives – and we're not talking fractions here. So, putting happiness at the top of the to-do list makes very good sense.

Yet the absence of sadness is not a sufficient criterion for happiness, just as the absence of illness is not one for health. Happiness, like health, is a distinctly positive state, it's not about getting by in neutral. Hence the emerging field of Positive Psychology, which is the scientific pursuit of the most promising routes for a distinctly happy and accomplished life.

This is certainly cheering stuff, because happiness certainly wasn't on the curriculum in my schooldays. In the coming weeks, this newspaper column will be examining just what this new discipline can tell us when it comes to pinpointing the skills and strategies, the experiences and environments, that can increase the likelihood of life feeling happier. It's worth a go because there's good evidence to suggest that our usual level of the feelgood factor can rise quite appreciably through our own efforts. But willingness is not enough, practical know-how is needed.

line 8
line 9
line 10

line 16
line 17

line 22

5   Which phrase is used to emphasise the weight of evidence supporting current views on happiness?

    A   we're not talking fractions here (lines 8–9)
    B   at the top of the to-do list (line 10)
    C   not about getting by in neutral (lines 16–17)
    D   this is certainly cheering stuff (line 22)

6   In this text, the writer is

    A   presenting a hypothesis which he will be testing.
    B   introducing the theme of a series of articles.
    C   encouraging people to take part in his research.
    D   presenting arguments for and against a theory.

Part 2

You are going to read an extract from a newspaper article. Six paragraphs have been removed from the extract. Choose from the paragraphs **A–G** the one which fits each gap (**7–12**). There is one extra paragraph which you do not need to use.
Mark your answers **on the separate answer sheet**.

A Change of Direction

Paul Roberts explains how he started writing CD-ROMs

It's Wednesday afternoon in Seattle and I'm writing about classical composers for a multimedia product on European history. I've never written about music before – my speciality, before I started writing CD-ROMs, was environmental journalism. But ignorance, in the new electronic age, isn't always an obstacle. The irony of the information revolution is that consumers neither like nor expect long, densely-written texts on their computer screens.

7

For example, of the 1,000 or so 'essays' I've written for CD-ROM companies over the last two years, fewer than 40 ran longer than 200 words and most were much, much shorter. I never expected to be working like this. I once earned a respectable living writing long, earnest articles about spotted owls, riverside ecology, even, on one occasion, a 10,000-word treatise on the Douglas Fir tree.

8

How malleable professional expectations are, particularly in the presence of cold cash, I would tell myself. For as I was beavering away on my alternative news weekly, I began to notice that many of my writer acquaintances were deserting ship in favour of the new CD-ROM phenomenon. I'd meet them at parties and they'd launch into breathless depictions of the *work* they were doing, and the *technology* they were using, and, more to the point, the buckets of money they were earning. It wasn't long before I had swallowed my principles and signed up for my first multimedia assignment.

A man called me at home and asked whether I had ever written for digital publications.

9

A year before, he'd been a magazine editor. Today, he seemed harassed and tired. He asked a few perfunctory questions about my writing, then, apparently satisfied, he moved on to a terse discussion of production schedules, software requirements and, finally, the Assignment, handing me a list of 50 subjects and a thick stack of reference materials.

10

I scanned his office, looking for clues as to what I'd got myself into. On the wall, I spied a chalk-board sketch, a series of small circles each labelled with an abbreviation ('Intro.', 'Vid.', 'Aud.') and all interconnected by spokes. A non-linear plan, he explained vaguely, waving at it. 'But you guys don't need to worry about that.' Very true. We writers simply get our assignments, write our texts and some months later, a shiny disc, wrapped in an inordinate amount of packaging, hits the bookshelves.

11

All that is handled by the engineers and designers who lay out the disc's schematic, who decide which digital object will be linked to which, and why. This prompts me to imagine a not-so-distant future when a sizeable fraction of professional writers won't ever enter the world of print but will go directly from school to digital publishing.

12	

Yet I can't help viewing this future with alarm and sadness, not simply because I question the

quality of the literature that people will have but because I can already see that I won't be capable of comprehending it. I have participated in, and in some small way precipitated, my own obsolescence.

A No one expects us to understand or care what happens to our texts before this happens. We needn't concern ourselves with story structure, or themes, or any of the other, more celebrated elements of traditional writing.

B I mumbled something ambiguous and found myself the following afternoon in a small beige office in a suburban megalopolis. The voice on the phone turned out to belong to the project producer, a gaunt fellow in his thirties whom I'll call Bob. We shook hands hastily.

C One of these was the routine demonstration of text's low rank on the **CD-ROM** totem pole; whenever software engineers had trouble cramming all the visual components onto a disc, writers would simply be told to chop texts in half.

D This is fast becoming a distant memory and nowadays I crank out little nuggets of information on whatever topics the multimedia companies believe will sell: dead large African mammals, yesterday's sports stars. It is, without question, hack writing, the kind of work (I used to think) only the unprincipled had the nerve to take.

E He wanted 75 words on each by the start of the following week. Nothing fancy. Simple declarative sentences. High-school reading level. Tight. No one had ever talked to me about writing like this and I felt disoriented.

F Maybe they'll be constrained at first by the needs of older readers who were raised on print. But in time this will change, as traditional printing comes to be seen as too expensive and cumbersome, and computers show up in every classroom and every living room worldwide.

G Such things slow down the rapid-fire 'interactive' process; and steal precious screen space from the animation, video and multimedia's other, more marketable, trivia. So we writers needn't be experts so much as filters, who compress reams of information into small easily-digestible, on-screen chunks.

Part 3

You are going to read a magazine article. For questions **13–19**, choose the answer (**A**, **B**, **C** or **D**) which you think fits best according to the text.
Mark your answers **on the separate answer sheet**.

Travel without a camera

Photographer Rupert Watson reassesses the value of the camera.

It could have been anywhere, my first intentionally photo-free journey, but it just happened to be Ethiopia. Photographic paraphernalia can be a great physical burden. It may weigh anything from a few hundred grams to several kilos, depending on how seriously one approaches the business of picture-taking. On top of all this are the practical problems of continuing logistical support – whether to gamble on the disaster of exhausted batteries or take spares. Yet the real burden of photography is mental, not physical; it is the feeling of needing to take photographs, that because you have a camera you must use it.

In the first few days of camera-less travel, there are certainly moments of frustration at letting one great photograph after another go past – those rare conjunctions of light and subject which create scenes of celluloid perfection. Yet having no camera, and thus being unable to take photographs, surprisingly soon stifles the urge to do so. Very quickly, scenes become appreciated for what they are, rather than for the photographs they would have made.

Climbing up the western wall of the Great Rift Valley, on the way to the capital, Addis Ababa, the road emerges from a tunnel onto open, grassy plains – a small piece of uncharacteristically undomesticated countryside, with an even more uncharacteristic population of wild mammals. These are Gelada baboons, herbivorous monkeys with hairless patches on their chests. They looked magnificent in the tearing wind, and through binoculars they could be indulged in at leisure – theirs and mine. And thus unseen, I watched their play, free from concerns as to how close I could risk going with my camera without losing the very moment I sought to capture for posterity.

Exciting though stalking wild creatures can be, the photographer must obviously stalk as much out of sight as possible, thus being denied any chance of actually watching them. The photographer's mind is effectively barred from experiencing any more than the photographic possibilities of the scene. At eye level, the camera not only creates a physical barrier but also isolates the photographer from the joyful reality of the subject, and from everywhere else around them too. Then comes the climax, the press of the button, the pull of the trigger, before more stalking, more photographs and, inevitably, the stalk too far which frightens the animals to flight. The difference between looking in order to photograph and actually seeing what is there is never more distinct than when taking pictures of animals, to the extent that the two become almost mutually exclusive. There is time only for deciding the best way to take the photograph, before addressing more mundane technicalities – how to keep the minibus's wheel out of the shot of lions, or get enough depth of field so all the flamingos on the lake are in focus at once.

While photographing scenery is an innocuous pastime which leaves few scars on the landscape, photographing people, animals, even buildings, can be a very selfish process. It takes much and gives little – except sometimes money and often offence. Some cultures feel genuinely intruded upon by photographers, and over-photographed animals are often disturbed to the point of deserting their young or missing their prey. For photographers, the story of the interaction with their subjects has a different ending, and they scuttle away to recreate a few frozen moments in the easy comfort of their sitting rooms. After the rounds of polite congratulation, the bundle of memories is then stuffed into a drawer, often never to be looked at again. Having no camera allowed me the luxury of being able to indulge in the sights, sounds and smells of Africa, without worrying if a flash might scare off the beasts, or the mouldering pile of background refuse might ruin the shot.

Of course great photography is an art, be it all too often an intrusive one. It is mindless photography that is so inane and inconsiderate, serving both to disturb its subjects and to diminish the richness of the journey. I can
line 40 hear rumbling accusations of selfishness and misanthropy. So be it – there is a price to pay for everything. The only picture I have of my girlfriend Mary Ann peering over a beautiful old Portuguese-inspired bridge over a narrow stretch of the Blue Nile is a mental one. True, it will fade faster than the photograph would have done; so will the image of the ears of a dozen donkeys poking above the edge of the bridge's parapet. But right now, any such regrets will have to wait. I'm chucking in banal holiday snapping, and leaving photography to others. I'll buy the guidebook and the picture postcards, and try to tread lightly on the lives of the people and creatures I travel amongst. Maybe then I'll finally start to see what I'm looking at.

13   According to the first paragraph, what is the main problem that photographers face while travelling?

    A   moving their heavy equipment about
    B   locating places to purchase accessories
    C   trying to get the best possible shots
    D   being under pressure to take photographs

14   The writer suggests in the second paragraph that people who choose to leave their cameras at home

    A   rapidly lose the desire to take any photographs.
    B   come to consider previous trips as unsatisfactory.
    C   appreciate the excellence of other people's photos.
    D   conclude that the decision was unrealistic.

15   What does the writer suggest about the monkeys he sees?

    A   They might have been enjoying the situation far more than he was.
    B   They were surprisingly unaffected by the close proximity of humans.
    C   They were too far away to be usefully observed.
    D   They might have become alarmed by the presence of a photographer.

16   The writer questions the value of stalking animals because a photographer

    A   can cause the animals to behave aggressively towards people.
    B   may become too uncomfortable to take reasonable shots.
    C   can easily become distracted from his task.
    D   may not be able to appreciate the situation fully.

17   In the fifth paragraph, the writer is casting doubt upon

    A   the long-term value of photographic images to those who take them.
    B   the assumption that people are willing to be photographed for free.
    C   the view that only the best photographs have aesthetic value.
    D   the belief that certain kinds of photography are harmful.

18   When he refers to 'rumbling accusations of selfishness and misanthropy' in line 40, the writer is

    A   denying an assumption.
    B   pointing out a flaw in an argument.
    C   anticipating a possible criticism.
    D   explaining a familiar misunderstanding.

19   The writer mentions his girlfriend to illustrate his view that

    A   the best memories are those that are shared.
    B   photography is the only way to record special events.
    C   abandoning photography can have its drawbacks.
    D   photographs can sometimes distort memories.

Part 4

You are going to read a newspaper article. For questions **20–34**, choose from the reviews (**A–D**).
The reviews may be chosen more than once.
Mark your answers **on the separate answer sheet**.

Which review mentions the following?

an initial concern that the book's purpose has been compromised for the sake of its visual appeal	20
an insight into a person's background	21
the view that a similar work of this scope is unlikely to be written	22
the undeserved reputation of species described in the book	23
an apparent contradiction between an outcome and the preparation for it	24
the fact that books of this kind have risked insulting the intelligence of the reader	25
the reviewer's confidence in the long-lasting significance of the work	26
the unconventional presentation of the content	27
the fact that this book makes little reference to the author's method	28
the considerable number of acknowledgements made to other written sources	29
the view that the book's overall quality is not affected by minor errors	30
the reviewer's belief that the book has successfully achieved a very difficult task	31
a certain imbalance in the consideration given to some aspects of the subject matter	32
the extent to which certain species are under threat	33
a preoccupation with the harm done by non-native species	34

Reviews of Wildlife Books

A   Introduced Mammals of the World: by John L. Long

This is a massive compilation – and probably the last time a single author will be able to undertake a comprehensive review in a single volume. John Long was an Australian, and his history of mammals introduced from elsewhere into that area is detailed and thorough. But British and European naturalists seeking a definitive reference work might be disappointed at the erratic coverage of their regions, as will many scientists, since a rather large proportion of the references are to other publications.

But anyone who decides to buy this will realise that these are small criticisms of a very valuable resource. Each species is covered under the following headings: description, distribution, habitat and behaviour, history of introductions, and damage to the area into which they were brought. The author's interest – and our current worldwide concerns – are reflected in the coverage of the damage that most alien introductions cause. There is no doubt that this book will remain a standard reference work for many years to come.

B   The New Encyclopedia of Insects and Their Allies: edited by Christopher O'Toole

Insects are the most numerous, most varied, most diverse and arguably the most important creatures on Planet Earth. For an encyclopedia to encompass such a broad slice of creation is a tall order indeed. For many, including myself, the idea of an encyclopedia is of a heavy tome of dense small type – useful for checking the odd fact or getting background to a new subject, but not really a riveting read. The publisher, Oxford University Press, certainly has the academic gravitas to carry out such a serious project, but its new animal encyclopedias are nothing if not colourful and popularist. Yes, the book is large and heavy, but its bright format owes more to magazine style than to reference-book layout.

Too often, popularising a subject has meant a patronising tone and inane commentary, which is ultimately counterproductive when trying to turn someone's attention to something new. But any such fears here are soon dispelled as even though the book is design-led and undoubtedly attractive, this has not stopped the injection of a large store of fact and detailed comment. Facts begin each chapter, with a list of basic headings on size, numbers and life cycle. Here too comes a short statement on conservation status – how many of each insect group are vulnerable, endangered or worse. As far as I am concerned, the tall order has been completed in full.

C   The New Encyclopedia of Reptiles and Amphibians: edited by Tim Halliday and Kraig Adler

This reference book is very attractive, and the artwork is not just pleasing to look at but is relevant to the text. There is a comprehensive overview of all the families, with drawings of representative species, together with distribution maps.

As with all works of this sort, it is fairly easy to pick up a few small inaccuracies (for instance, the description of midwife toads and frogs mentions a species native to the Middle East, but only shows the family as occurring in the western Mediterranean), but this does not detract from a generally well-produced and up-to-date work of reference. Buy it because these creatures are, whatever the widespread misconceptions, some of the most exciting and interesting animals alive today.

D   Birds and Light: by Lars Jonsson

This book has lots to say about Jonsson's creative approach, as well as being full of fabulous drawings, sketches and paintings of birds. His images are full of life – he manages to perfectly capture a moment in time and also reveal a profound understanding of the subject and its surroundings. Paradoxically, artwork that captures the 'momentary' requires serious groundwork and the artist must take time to set it up. It is this aspect of Jonsson's work that forms the bulk of the text. He doesn't reveal much about *how* he works; just, for example, that he uses a good telescope and thin watercolours, and shelters from the wind. But much more interesting is *what* we discover about him: his studying of the work of great figures in art history and his lifelong passion for bird identification are also part of his groundwork.

PAPER 2   WRITING (1 hour 30 minutes)

Part 1

You **must** answer this question. Write your answer in **180–220** words in an appropriate style.

---

1   You are Secretary of the Film Club at your English language college. The Principal of the college has concerns about the club's popularity and has asked you for information.

Read the memo from the Principal below and the club notice, on which you have made some notes. Then, **using the information appropriately**, write a proposal for the Principal, saying what aspects of the club are successful, recommending ways to resolve any problems and explaining why the college should continue to fund the club.

To:	Film Club
From:	Principal

The college pays a lot of money to fund the club when it has very few members. If you cannot come up with any suggestions, I may have to reduce the funding.

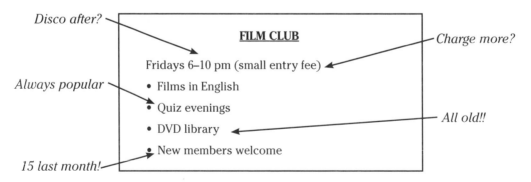

Disco after?

FILM CLUB

Charge more?

Fridays 6–10 pm (small entry fee)

Always popular

• Films in English

• Quiz evenings

• DVD library

All old!!

• New members welcome

15 last month!

Write your **proposal**. You should use your own words as far as possible.

Part 2

Write an answer to **one** of the questions **2–5** in this part. Write your answer in **220–260** words in an appropriate style.

---

2   In your English class, you have been talking about how television affects children. Your teacher has asked you to write an essay on the following subject:

Television has both negative and positive effects on children. Do you agree?

Write your **essay**.

3   You read the following announcement in an international magazine.

> **'Person of the Year' Competition**
>
> Who do you think deserves this title?
> Write and tell us about the person who has contributed the most to making the year memorable. You must justify your choice by explaining what the person's contribution has been and why the person will be remembered.

Write your **competition entry**.

4   You see this announcement on a student website.

> On our website we are collecting reviews of magazines which are popular with young people. We invite you to submit a review of a magazine you know well which is read by young people. Your review should describe briefly the types of article which appear in the magazine, explain why the magazine is popular with young people and suggest how it could be improved.

Write your **review**.

5   Answer **one** of the following two questions based on **one** of the titles below.

(a) *Through a Glass, Darkly* by Donna Leon

Your teacher has asked you to write a report on the importance of family in *Through a Glass, Darkly*. Your report should explain the attitude of Tassini towards his family and say how his attitude influences his behaviour in the story.

Write your **report**.

(b) *Of Mice and Men* by John Steinbeck

In class, you have been discussing *Of Mice and Men*. Your teacher has asked you to write an essay on the following subject:

George is the most likeable character in Of Mice and Men. *To what extent do you agree?*

Write your **essay**.

PAPER 3   USE OF ENGLISH (1 hour)

Part 1

For questions **1–12**, read the text below and decide which answer (**A, B, C** or **D**) best fits each gap. There is an example at the beginning (**0**).
Mark your answers **on the separate answer sheet**.

Example:

0 A schemes   **B** points   **C** ends   **D** aims

0	A	B	C	D
	☐	☐	☐	▬

Responding to children's mistakes

Promoting children's self-esteem seems to be one of the **(0)** …….. of modern childcare and education. It goes hand in hand with a culture in which children are **(1)** …….. praised for the most **(2)** …….. achievements. While this promotion of self-esteem is, rightly, a reaction against sterner times when children weren't praised enough, it also seems to be **(3)** …….. by a fear of how failure will affect children: a fear that if they don't succeed at a task, they will somehow be damaged.

However, the opposite may well be true. Many scientists spend years experiencing **(4)** …….. failure in the lab until they make a **(5)** …….. . They know that **(6)** …….. this process advances scientific knowledge. In the same way, children need to experience failure to learn and grow. If children have been praised for everything they've done, **(7)** …….. how good it is, then failure in adult life will be all the more painful.

Life is full of **(8)** …….. and there is no point in trying to protect children from the disappointments that **(9)** …….. them. Parents and educators shouldn't be afraid of **(10)** …….. children's mistakes, as long as they also praise them when they do well. After all, the heroes children try to **(11)** …….. , the pop stars and footballers, have all reached the top in the face of ruthless competition. Like them, children need to learn how to cope with failure and **(12)** …….. it to their advantage.

1 **A** immensely   **B** enthusiastically   **C** thoroughly   **D** devotedly

2 **A** minor   **B** inferior   **C** miniature   **D** light

3 **A** developed   **B** evolved   **C** caused   **D** originated

4 **A** concurrent   **B** consequent   **C** consecutive   **D** continual

5 **A** success   **B** breakthrough   **C** progress   **D** breakout

6 **A** ultimately   **B** lastly   **C** conclusively   **D** latterly

7 **A** according to   **B** regardless of   **C** consistent with   **D** depending on

8 **A** faults   **B** checks   **C** delays   **D** setbacks

9 **A** expect   **B** anticipate   **C** await   **D** approach

10 **A** getting round to   **B** looking down on   **C** giving way to   **D** picking up on

11 **A** simulate   **B** duplicate   **C** emulate   **D** replicate

12 **A** move   **B** turn   **C** make   **D** take

Part 2

For questions **13–27**, read the text below and think of the word which best fits each gap. Use only **one** word in each gap. There is an example at the beginning (**0**).

Write your answers **IN CAPITAL LETTERS on the separate answer sheet**.

Example:

0	W	A	S															

Whistling

When **(0)** …….. the last time you heard someone whistling a tune? It used to be commonplace, a natural thing to do **(13)** …….. walking or washing the car. **(14)** …….. , however, it's quite rare to hear this simple kind of music.

No-one really knows **(15)** …….. it should be that whistling has lost its popularity, **(16)** …….. one anthropology professor thinks that portable music technology could be **(17)** …….. blame for its disappearance. **(18)** …….. seems little point in whistling when your iPod can play the tune for you! Another theory is that present-day tunes are just **(19)** …….. attractive to whistlers – it's hard to find a melody to follow.

Some people say that it's impossible to whistle **(20)** …….. you're happy, while others boast **(21)** …….. the mood-elevating qualities whistling has. What's more, sustained spells of whistling **(22)** …….. also thought to exercise the stomach muscles and lungs. There are some people who claim they cannot whistle at all **(23)** …….. it's true that it takes practice to master the technique. However, these people are probably trying **(24)** …….. hard and should blow more gently.

But there's **(25)** …….. side to whistling. It's not only a musical art and a physical exercise, it's also a means of communication, through **(26)** …….. a message is conveyed. This is particularly useful for communication that needs to take place over a distance, as the sound of a whistle **(27)** …….. travel further than ordinary speech. In one mountain village in southern Europe, for example, the entire population regularly whistles, and they frequently hold whistled conversations.

Part 3

For questions **28–37**, read the text below. Use the word given in capitals at the end of some of the lines to form a word that fits in the gap **in the same line**. There is an example at the beginning **(0)**.

Write your answers **IN CAPITAL LETTERS on the separate answer sheet**.

Example:

0	C	O	M	B	I	N	A	T	I	O	N					

Kite surfing

I recently travelled to the Red Sea resort of Abu Soma to try kite surfing, the

world's newest extreme sport. I'd heard that the **(0)** .... of strong winds   **COMBINE**

from the desert and the calm lagoon waters mean the conditions are ideal

for beginners. The **(28)** .... of expert instruction made it the perfect choice   **AVAILABLE**

for my holiday.

My instructor, Dan Silver, explained that kite surfing was invented by the

French in the 1990s and **(29)** .... by surfers in Hawaii. 'You can master the   **POPULAR**

basics in a few days,' he told me, 'although you need longer to learn how to

do acrobatics.'

My first task was learning how to **(30)** .... the immensely powerful kite   **HAND**

on land and it was with some **(31)** .... that I allowed Dan to hook it onto   **RELUCTANT**

my harness. I was **(32)** .... of being dragged into the sea by the kite.   **TERROR**

(33) .... , however, there are ways to release the kite in an emergency.   **THANK**

Once in the water, I felt safer. The board has footholds to **(34)** .... your   **SURE**

feet don't slip off and Is designed to maintain **(35)** .... at high speed. I'm a   **STABLE**

good snowboarder, and my **(36)** .... in this sport definitely helped. Soon,   **EXPERT**

I began to find kite surfing **(37)** .... and started wondering when I could   **ADDICT**

return to Abu Soma for more.

Part 4

For questions **38–42**, think of **one** word only which can be used appropriately in all three sentences. Here is an example (**0**).

Example:

0 They say the new minister is a lovely person and very ……………….. to talk to.

My neighbours have not had a very ……………….. life, but they always seem cheerful.

It's ……………….. enough to see why the town is popular with tourists.

Example:

0	E	A	S	Y														

Write **only** the missing word **IN CAPITAL LETTERS on the separate answer sheet**.

---

38 As part of the camping skills course, boy scouts will learn how to use ……………….. safely.

The lawyer pointed out that there were simply no ……………….. between the DNA samples found at the crime scene and the DNA of her clients.

Because of this weekend's wet weather, both semi-final ……………….. have been postponed until next weekend.

39 I used to hate living in a large city, but I've ……………….. to like it now.

Over the last decade, Flint's reputation as a film director has ……………….. considerably.

I've ……………….. some fantastic flowers and vegetables in my garden this year.

40 Extensive studies have shown that no ……………….. of life can exist on the planet Mercury, as daytime temperatures are too high.

The houses on the new estate will be laid out in the ……………….. of a semi-circle.

After you have completed the ……………….. , please return it to the university in the envelope provided.

41 I .... aside some money each month until I had enough to buy a nice camera.

When the children didn't understand what the teacher said, she .... it more simply.

The mechanic .... the cost of fixing the car at about £450.

42 I had to return the dress I bought because, once I got it home, I realised it was just too ....

Security had to be very .... as the event involved so many important heads of state.

Although employees were used to working to .... schedules, they knew that they would have to do overtime to meet the latest deadline.

Part 5

For questions **43–50**, complete the second sentence so that it has a similar meaning to the first sentence, using the word given. **Do not change the word given.** You must use between **three** and **six** words, including the word given. Here is an example (**0**).

Example:

0 James would only speak to the head of department alone.

ON

James .... to the head of department alone.

The gap can be filled with the words 'insisted on speaking', so you write:

Example: | **0** | INSISTED ON SPEAKING

Write **only** the missing words **IN CAPITAL LETTERS on the separate answer sheet**.

---

43 Although Grace travels a lot, she's always forgetting her passport.

FIRST

Although Grace travels a lot, this .... that she's forgotten her passport.

44 You'll still have to pay the technician for looking at your computer, even if he says it is beyond repair.

CAN

Whether your computer .... not, you'll still have to pay the technician for looking at it.

45 I had no success in contacting Colin before the party.

MANAGE

I .... hold of Colin before the party.

46   Everyone in my football club is sure that Portugal will win the final against England.

BEATEN

Everyone in my football club is sure that England ………………………………… the final.

47   Hardly any boys among my students know who Virginia Woolf is.

HEARD

Among my students, very ………………………………… Virginia Woolf.

48   Harry was going to take his mother for a drive in his new sports car but it looks as if he's forgotten.

MUST

Harry ………………………………… taking his mother for a drive in his new sports car.

49   Charlotte definitely didn't intend to return to the house until all the building work had been done.

INTENTION

Charlotte had absolutely ………………………………… to the house until all the building work had been done.

50   Mr Wang thought that Japanese was going to be an easy language for him to learn.

IMPRESSION

Mr Wang was ………………………………… be easy for him to learn Japanese.

PAPER 4   LISTENING (approximately 40 minutes)

Part 1

You will hear three different extracts. For questions **1–6**, choose the answer (**A, B** or **C**) which fits best according to what you hear. There are two questions for each extract.

Extract One

You overhear a football fan talking to a friend about a new stadium he's just been to.

1 He thinks the architect's decision not to use strong colours was good because

    A the stadium has to blend in with its surroundings.

    B it gives the stadium a more sophisticated atmosphere.

    C the matches and crowds will provide a feeling of energy.

2 He compares the new stadium to a modern airport in order to

    A praise the quality of the facilities.

    B emphasise the size of the building.

    C explain how many people it can hold.

Extract Two

You hear part of an interview with the presenter of a breakfast radio programme.

3 How does she feel about her job?

    A keen to continue as long as she can

    B fearful that she will soon be replaced

    C reluctant to go into work on some occasions

4 When talking about her colleague, she reveals

    A her amusement at his choice of language.

    B her admiration of what he can get away with.

    C her wish that she could be as popular as him.

Extract Three

You overhear two friends called Greg and Tamsin discussing a newspaper article about something called a seed bank.

5   According to Tamsin, what is the purpose of the seed bank?

    A to encourage farmers to sow older crop varieties

    B to ensure replacement of species which may be lost

    C to enable experts to produce disease-resistant plants

6   Greg thinks that the organisers of the seed bank

    A are underestimating the security issues.

    B will have difficulty finding the right personnel.

    C have not adequately specified the procedures involved.

Part 2

You will hear a musician called Barbara Devlin talking about the instrument she plays, which is called the penny whistle. For questions **7–14**, complete the sentences.

The penny whistle

For many centuries, whistles have been made of wood and

	7

Barbara says that tin was both

	8

and plentiful in the nineteenth century.

The only part of the penny whistle not made of metal is called the

	9

Robert Dark first sold his whistles in villages which had a

	10

Many of Robert Dark's whistles were taken to

	11

, where whistles had always been popular.

Robert Dark's factory was close to the

	12

in Manchester.

Barbara says that the breath marks in penny-whistle sheet music shouldn't be regarded as

	13

Barbara compares the breath marks in penny-whistle sheet music to the

	14

in a piece of writing.

Part 3

You will hear an interview with an underwater photographer called Adam Pigot, who is talking about his work. For questions **15–20**, choose the answer (**A**, **B**, **C** or **D**) which fits best according to what you hear.

15   Adam first became attracted to underwater diving through

    A being involved in the film world as a child.
    B doing his training when he was in the army.
    C talking to his colleagues while working as a cameraman.
    D responding to requests for unusual photographs at meetings.

16   Adam says he is given advertising work by sportswear manufacturers because

    A he has been a keen sportsman all his life.
    B he has some experience as a sports photographer.
    C he is willing to experiment with photographic techniques.
    D he is generally more available than other photographers.

17   When selecting the team he works with underwater, Adam is

    A told the number of people he can have with him.
    B determined to have assistants with experience.
    C concerned about contradicting his superiors.
    D willing to give young people an opportunity.

18   How does Adam feel about working with a team at sea?

    A The safety requirements are too relaxed.
    B The lack of communication makes him nervous.
    C The risks involved have to be acknowledged.
    D The mishaps that occur are often exaggerated.

19   According to Adam, working in a deep water tank in the studio

    A produces less exciting images.
    B can cause disputes within the team.
    C exposes the team to health hazards.
    D requires the use of expensive equipment.

20   Adam dislikes using artificial light underwater because

    A it puts too much strain on his budget.
    B it does not show the models at their best.
    C it lacks sufficient power to give the required effect.
    D it makes his working conditions too unpredictable.

Part 4

You will hear five short extracts in which young people are talking about going shopping for clothes.

TASK ONE

For questions **21–25**, choose from the list (**A–H**) the reason each speaker gives for going clothes shopping.

TASK TWO

For questions **26–30**, choose from the list (**A–H**) the aspect of going clothes shopping that each speaker most enjoys.

While you listen you must complete both tasks.

A	receiving a pay rise	**A** getting a bargain
B	a friend's suggestion	**B** seeing the latest designs
C	a change in the weather	**C** the chance to meet up with friends
D	a change in weight	**D** the atmosphere in the town centre
E	a change of hairstyle	**E** changing their personal image
F	preparing for a special occasion	**F** being in control of decision-making
G	reading a fashion magazine	**G** getting professional advice
H	replacing worn-out items	**H** the journey home with their purchases

Speaker 1 | 21
Speaker 2 | 22
Speaker 3 | 23
Speaker 4 | 24
Speaker 5 | 25

Speaker 1 | 26
Speaker 2 | 27
Speaker 3 | 28
Speaker 4 | 29
Speaker 5 | 30

PAPER 5   SPEAKING (15 minutes)

There are two examiners. One (the interlocutor) conducts the test, providing you with the necessary materials and explaining what you have to do. The other examiner (the assessor) is introduced to you, but then takes no further part in the interaction.

Part 1 (3 minutes)

The interlocutor first asks you and your partner a few questions. The interlocutor asks candidates for some information about themselves, then widens the scope of the questions by asking about e.g. candidates' leisure activities, studies, travel and daily life. Candidates are expected to respond to the interlocutor's questions and listen to what their partner has to say.

Part 2 (a one-minute 'long turn' for each candidate, plus a 30-second response from the second candidate)

You are each given the opportunity to talk for about a minute, and to comment briefly after your partner has spoken.

The interlocutor gives you a set of pictures and asks you to talk about them for about one minute. It is important to listen carefully to the interlocutor's instructions. The interlocutor then asks your partner a question about your pictures and your partner responds briefly.

You are then given another set of pictures to look at. Your partner talks about these pictures for about one minute. This time the interlocutor asks you a question about your partner's pictures and you respond briefly.

Part 3 (approximately 4 minutes)

In this part of the test, you and your partner are asked to talk together. The interlocutor places a new set of pictures on the table between you. This stimulus provides the basis for a discussion. The interlocutor explains what you have to do.

Part 4 (approximately 4 minutes)

The interlocutor asks some further questions, which leads to a more general discussion of what you have talked about in Part 3. You may comment on your partner's answers if you wish.

Test 3

PAPER 1 READING (1 hour 15 minutes)

Part 1

You are going to read three extracts which are all concerned in some way with the brain. For questions **1–6**, choose the answer (**A, B, C** or **D**) which you think fits best according to the text. Mark your answers **on the separate answer sheet**.

Advertisement

Brain Training Courses

Caroline Simmons, our expert in all things brain- and learning-related, returns in December with the first of a new season of courses on mind mapping and speed reading.

MIND MAPPING

Significantly, modern studies confirm that creativity is not a rare gift of the chosen few but a series of cognitive skills that can be taught, harnessed and applied. And when such skills are developed effectively, the possibilities for individuals to expand their minds, create, manage and lead are infinite. On the course about Mind Mapping, invented by Tony Buzan, you will experience the full breadth of Caroline's knowledge and expertise about the subject, and use Buzan's groundbreaking iMindMap software. This is a brilliant method of creating, harnessing and presenting big ideas and strategies to any audience ... from your immediate family or school to packed arenas of students or business leaders.

SPEED READING

Again based on Tony Buzan's work, Caroline outlines how your eyes and brain absorb and retain information, offering practical techniques and exercises so that you can put your new skills to use straight away. Discover powerful techniques that can increase your reading speed up to tenfold, without compromising understanding. Glean and remember the key points from any written material in a fraction of the time it would usually take, learning to read at a range of speeds appropriate to the material ... from detailed creative appreciation of poetry to rapid, strategic assimilation of a report.

1   We find out from the paragraph on Mind Mapping that

   A   the course will be of most benefit to specific people.
   B   the software has been developed over time.
   C   Buzan's techniques are being used by businesses.
   D   Buzan's ideas have been incorporated into an innovative product.

2   The advertisement says that speed reading

   A   is being applied to new subject areas.
   B   does not lead to a decline in comprehension.
   C   enables users to remember facts for longer.
   D   is a skill which takes time for users to assimilate effectively.

Research into memory

People with greater working-memory capacity may be able to suppress unwanted memories, according to Chris Brewin of University College London. He says that the process of inhibiting memories, or forgetting, uses up mental resources – that forgetting is an active rather than a passive process – and that it is surprisingly important for useful brain function. Many of our everyday memories aren't lost or thrown away, they are just merged. As time passes, the details drop away and only the broad outlines remain. You don't remember every breakfast you ate as a child, but you will remember those foods you habitually ate or never liked. In other words, you remember the gist of breakfast past.

Barry Gordon of Johns Hopkins University likens human memory to the 'lossy' system used in MP3 music files. Information that's not essential is deleted and what's left is compressed. Gordon believes that this process of forgetting is crucial if the brain is to generate new ideas – that remembering too much detail prevents you from seeing the pattern. He has noticed that some people with fantastic memories for detail lament the fact that they never have original thoughts. It could just be that they can't see the wood for the trees.

3   The example of breakfast illustrates the fact that

   A   we can access distant memories.
   B   the brain chooses to recall certain details.
   C   the brain compensates for lost information.
   D   we can remember main ideas but not details.

4   Barry Gordon's work suggests that forgetting

   A   is an aid to creativity.
   B   is a conscious process.
   C   has no predetermined pattern.
   D   can inhibit certain thought processes.

Extract from a novel

Two thoughts at once

Your brain can only have one thought at any time. We accept this as normal because we're so used to it. But when you consider how many million memories our brains can store with ease, it's surprising that we can only think one thing at a time. It's like an expensive car whose windscreen washer works fine – but not if the engine's running. What on earth are a gazillion unused synapses doing at any one time? Redecorating? Dozing?

That's what people believe, anyway. Personally, I'm not so sure. I think I'm capable of having two or more thoughts simultaneously. I'm not talking about 'beliefs'. You can believe many things about one subject, even mutually contradictory things, at the same time. But beliefs, like memories, are what you 'hold'; and you only become aware of them when you explain, revise or put them into words. Everyone does that.

What I can do is have two or more conscious thoughts at once. It's as though my conscious brain has a split screen. Generally, of course, there's just one picture; but frequently there are two. Each has its own soundtrack, each exists and runs happily at its own pace and I am equally conscious of each. Occasionally, my screen redivides and I think three or four things at the same time. More than that, however, is troublesome and there comes a moment when I ask myself what I'm doing. Then all the thoughts tumble, like the batons of a juggler who has become self-conscious.

5   In the second paragraph, what does the writer say about beliefs?

   A   People are not always conscious of their beliefs.
   B   People do not usually have internally-conflicting beliefs.
   C   People base their beliefs on their memories of past experiences.
   D   People have difficulty in adequately expressing their beliefs.

6   In the third paragraph, the writer refers to the juggler in order to indicate

   A   the danger involved when he concentrates on one thought.
   B   the concentration needed to sustain simultaneous thoughts.
   C   the training he has had to undertake to think multiple thoughts.
   D   the trouble his unusual talent causes for people around him.

Part 2

You are going to read an extract from a magazine article. Six paragraphs have been removed from the extract. Choose from the paragraphs **A–G** the one which fits each gap (**7–12**). There is one extra paragraph which you do not need to use.
Mark your answers **on the separate answer sheet**.

CONFESSIONS OF A BAD LOSER

When the World One-Day Novel-Writing Competition was held recently, freelance journalist and author James Delingpole was invited to take part. The winner has just been announced – and it's not him. Here he describes his reaction.

If I sound bitter, it's because I am. Tonight, had justice been done, I should have been named as the winner of the world's second 24-hour novel-writing competition.

7 [   ]

I know what one is meant to say when faced with such failure. 'Nothing ventured, nothing gained. It's not the winning but the taking part that counts.' Personally, though, I've never had much time for sporting comments such as these. And when I enter a competition, I want to win, effortlessly and by the widest possible margin. I want to be famous. I want to be rich.

8 [   ]

But that wasn't an option, and so it was that at 10 a.m. on the brightest, sunniest Saturday this year, I found myself entombed in a room full of word processors and TV crews with, among others, a 14-year-old schoolboy, a university chemistry student and at least one other journalist, bashing out my first sentence.

9 [   ]

Four hours, five cups of coffee and half a dozen cigarettes later, I'd finally hit my stride. I could overlook such minor inconveniences as the accidental erasure of my original first chapter (someone tripped over a cable) and the fact that, contrary to my inflated predictions to a TV

cameraman earlier in the day, I was averaging a mere 500 words an hour. What mattered was that, having sorted out those time-consuming passages designed to impress the competition judges in Chapter One, I had turned my attentions to the brilliant intricacies of my plot.

10 [   ]

And writing *Hell on Wheels* (the punchy title I chose, with an eye on future publication) was fun. Up to a point. I relished the adrenalised thrill of an urgent deadline. I enjoyed the nervy banter with my rivals during those fleeting breaks ('How many words so far?' 'What!? You're kidding!'); and, above all, having only recently finished a 'proper' novel which took four years to plot, three months to draft and another eighteen months to revise, I found the chance to condense that whole experience into an intensive period of frenzied creativity joyously liberating.

11 [   ]

Yet I did it. By the 23rd hour I had completed my 12,000-word story. And when, an hour later, I had finished my cursory corrections, I slumped in my chair – shattered by exhilaration – and began planning my acceptance speech.

12 [   ]

My speech would have been long, insincere and very boring. So too, no doubt, would this article!

A This is something of an understatement. Scarcely can the description do justice to my tale of mysterious disappearances, dark conspiracies and breathless adventure, all set in an imaginary future. My main aim during the two 12-hour shifts was to come up with a story which required no research and which I would find entertaining to write.

B That, at any rate, was the outcome my editor had in mind when she commissioned this article from me ten days ago. Instead, I am slowly coming to terms with the fact that not only did I fail to beat my 50 or so fellow entrants – I didn't even make the shortlist of seven.

C Such accounts of failure make for more enjoyable reading than modest reports of victory. And who, in any case, would ever be so foolish as to desire a full-time literary career? Everyone knows there's no money in novels any more.

D I think it was the bit about not having to work too hard that appealed to me most when I accepted the assignment just a day and a half before the competition was due to start. Given two months' notice, I might well have turned it down.

E That said, it was not an ordeal I should care to repeat. Sleep was virtually impossible both on the Saturday night and on the Sunday when it was all over – and when it came, I was haunted by my fictive creations. My eyes stung, my head throbbed and I could barely speak an intelligible sentence.

F I would pay magnanimous tribute to my rivals' endurance and remarkable friendliness; I would protest at how undeserving my victory had been when so many other entrants had staked their whole careers on winning the competition.

G 'Even above the laughter of the club regulars', this began, before dissolving into a wordless void which would not be filled for a good half-hour. Clever, attention-grabbing openings are always the trickiest part, I thought, trying to ignore the fluent pitter-patter of my rivals' keyboards.

Part 3

You are going to read an extract from an autobiography. For questions **13–19**, choose the answer (**A**, **B**, **C** or **D**) which you think fits best according to the text.
Mark your answers **on the separate answer sheet**.

COMING HOME IN MASSACHUSETTS

by Simon Winchester

Last week a man with a flat-bed trailer came to take away my tractor, to fit it with a backhoe. This sentence, which I found myself writing yesterday in an email home to my parents, is not one I could have ever imagined myself even thinking of writing, as little as a year ago. Then I lived a somewhat dashing existence, roaming the remoter parts of the planet or, when settled, inhabiting a world of costly apartments in capital cities, fancy cafés and edgy urban chatter. I wasn't at all sure what a flat-bed trailer was, and certainly had no idea of the functions of a backhoe! Tractors were merely burbling little machines that chugged around in farmers' fields in that curious 'beyond' one saw from train windows, known as 'the country'. The notion that I'd ever own or want to own one, or live among those to whom they were a customary form of transport, was outside my powers of imagination.

Well, that was then and this is now. Now I own a tractor and last week a man with a flat-bed trailer came to take it away, to fix it up with a backhoe, something which weighs half a ton, needs greasing every week and costs a very great deal more than I expected. And all this has happened because, after many fairly exciting, exacting, sophisticated and mainly metropolitan years, I have voluntarily become a country dweller. It is a role I find I have slipped into as easily as a deerskin work-glove, and in doing so I have become inordinately happy.

The notion of settling anywhere was to me once utterly alien. I was 16 when I began to travel seriously; I hitchhiked the entire circumference of populated North America one summer, and it was then that I developed a taste for the risks and rewards of solitary wandering. Over the following years, thanks to the indulgence of a number of newspaper editors, I lived in (or, perhaps more appropriately, I was based in) Africa, India, Ireland, China and the United States. I believe I travelled to almost every country on the planet. I have had more homes than I can remember, more telephone numbers, more email addresses; and friends who are kind enough to keep me in their address books grumble at the 'W' page, dominated by so many rubbings-out and fillings-in. Can't you settle down? they ask in kindly-weary exasperation. Of course, they add, we envy you mightily. And for a while I thought they did, especially if their lives depended on catching commuter trains and sitting in offices looking forward to games of golf at weekends. Except that the life of the fancy-free was often much more fancy than free.

And as my years began to tick on I confess that I began to ponder such matters and wonder at the supposed benefits of endless wanderings. This feeling gradually strengthened until, on a sudden whim last year, I bought a rambling old house and a plot of weary farmland in western Massachusetts. And in doing so I wondered if I too, a little late, might for the first time try settling down. It might work; it might not. But if it didn't, then at least it would be another adventure from which to make another anecdote. That was nine months ago. Since then, aside from two journeys to Java and a handful to Europe, I have not budged. Eight months ago, four weeks into the experiment, came an epiphany. It involved a tractor.

I mentioned that I now own a tractor. It came with the property. It is not as old as the house but it has done a half-century of yeoman service. It is a faded, rusty blue Ford. It needs to be cranked into life with much care and gentle words. But once so eased into mechanical vivacity it runs quite merrily, chugging and pulsing steadily like a heartbeat. Attached to its rear is a spinning blade. This is what people round here like to use to mow their fields. Not to make their lawns satin-smooth, but merely to get the thistles and weeds down to a height in which children and small animals don't get totally lost.

One warm evening, as the sun was setting, I decided to have a go. I sat on the machine, fired up the engine and set off unsteadily down the meadow. No sweeter smell have I ever known, in any place I have ever been: new-mown grass – new-mown hay, in fact, for what I was cutting was tall grass and blue alfalfa, which smells more unimaginably lovely than anything in the world. In that moment I was utterly hooked, totally transformed. It was as though, in that one instant, the earth sang out: Stay here. Dig holes here. Put down roots. Nurture them gently with sun and rain, until, like that old rusty blue Ford, they burble into life, and show that something that grows has more point than anything born from ceaseless wandering.

13   The writer mentions the recent modification to his tractor in order to emphasise

    A   his reliance on the willingness of local people to help him.
    B   the speed at which the countryside is changing.
    C   the contrast between his past life and his present one.
    D   his resentment at the high cost of living in the countryside.

14   What does the writer imply about his travels in the third paragraph?

    A   He had difficulty deciding where to base himself.
    B   There are few countries he still wants to visit.
    C   His early experiences made him prefer remote destinations.
    D   He was fortunate in being able to travel for his work.

15   What does the writer suggest about his friends in the third paragraph?

    A   They would not really have enjoyed his lifestyle.
    B   They were unreasonable in expecting him to settle down.
    C   They wished he would visit them more often.
    D   They were dissatisfied with the way they spent their free time.

16   What is the writer doing in the fourth paragraph?

    A   summing up his current feelings
    B   coming to terms with a change of heart
    C   explaining how he came to a decision
    D   emphasising the rightness of his new life

17   What does the writer say about his tractor in the fifth paragraph?

    A   It is the reason he bought the house.
    B   It is difficult to start but reliable.
    C   It is specially adapted for safety.
    D   It is mainly used for gardening.

18   In the final paragraph, the writer makes a comparison between the way the tractor operates and

    A   his attitude towards life on a farm.
    B   his initiation into working in the countryside.
    C   the joys of constantly travelling the world.
    D   the workings of nature.

19   In describing his experiences the writer is

    A   unsettled by his new environment.
    B   surprised at the change in himself.
    C   nostalgic for some places he has been to.
    D   confident about his future success.

Part 4

You are going to read an article about a young violinist. For questions **20–34**, choose from the sections **A–D**. The sections may be chosen more than once.
Mark your answers **on the separate answer sheet**.

Which section mentions

the fate of musicians who have followed similar career paths to Kuznetsov? | 20 |

a benefit of music that Kuznetsov believes deserves greater recognition? | 21 |

the fact that Kuznetsov's musical ability is far superior to that of other accomplished violinists? | 22 |

the extent to which Kuznetsov could play from memory? | 23 |

a concern that Kuznetsov's playing may lose a particular characteristic? | 24 |

the emphasis Kuznetsov places on the ability to build a relationship with other musicians? | 25 |

Kuznetsov never wavering in his musical ambitions? | 26 |

a misgiving that Kuznetsov shares with other talented musicians? | 27 |

how Kuznetsov thought people should regard the opportunity to hear him play? | 28 |

Kuznetsov's plan to extend his accomplishments being part of a logical progression for him? | 29 |

an element of Kuznetsov's playing that he feels has stayed the same? | 30 |

the time Kuznetsov takes to reflect on a piece of music? | 31 |

an occasion on which Kuznetsov managed to convey the meaning inherent in a piece of music? | 32 |

an opinion resulting from the confidence with which Kuznetsov played recently? | 33 |

Kuznetsov's reluctance to predict his own style? | 34 |

A New String to Leonid Kuznetsov's Bow

Paul Rogers reports on Leonid's transition from violinist to conductor

A

Giving a master class to young violinists in London, Leonid Kuznetsov creates theatre. The boy who thinks his job is merely to realise Mozart's marks on paper finds himself in the middle of a play with conspiratorial whispers and expressions of swooning love. Kuznetsov discovers the drama behind every phrase.

There have been other violin prodigies but none could hold a candle to this miraculous young Russian. On his emergence while still in his teens, Kuznetsov's playing was imbued with timeless wisdom beyond his years; he now holds the stage with immense and charismatic authority. So it comes as no surprise that he is about to add a new string to his bow. When he performs with the English Chamber Orchestra, it will be as both soloist and conductor. 'It's something I've often thought about,' he says. 'I've been feeling the need to share my music in new ways, and transmitting that with my hands and eyes seemed like the next step.'

B

Other musicians who have traded the bow or piano for the baton have vanished into obscurity; the transition has pitfalls, of which he is aware. 'The most crucial thing is the human chemistry between conductor and players. If it doesn't exist, you may as well give up. You must avoid at all costs being an outsider, as though saying to the orchestra, "You make your music while I imagine mine."'

He is quite relaxed about not yet having his own hand-language – every conductor is different. Kuznetsov believes the connection between notes is not just physical, but also spiritual. Spirituality is, for Kuznetsov, the conductor's key attribute. 'And it should ideally be expressed through beauty of movement,' he says. Some conductors hurl themselves about, others hardly move a muscle. Where will Kuznetsov fit on that scale? 'We must wait and see,' he says.

C

Kuznetsov himself moved straight as an arrow toward his goal. His father was an oboist and his mother conducted a choir, but at the age of four, young Leonid settled on the violin. 'The violin is located at the front of the orchestra. It seemed very desirable to sit there and show off.' Later, armed with a miniature violin, he and his mother gate-crashed their way into a lesson with the best teacher in town. 'In my fourth lesson, I played her 80 songs by heart, and she said to my mother, "We have a genius."'

He gave his first concert at the age of five. 'When I went on stage, I bowed so deeply and so long that the audience laughed – but I knew that this was what great artists always did. I felt it was a privilege for the audience to listen to me.' His programme that day included Paganini variations, 'which were very easy for me'.

What is his view now of the recordings he made at that age? 'It's incredible that a teacher could have achieved such things with someone so young. I didn't have the technique I have now but across the years the intuition has not changed. I still feel every time I go on stage as though I'm newborn.'

D

Kuznetsov cautiously paces his own development. He deferred his first performance of Beethoven's Violin Concerto until he felt ready for it, and he'll let Bach's sonatas marinate in his mind for some years. Like many great artists, he's uneasy about much contemporary music – 'I find it difficult to understand the harmony.'

He believes that classical music needs greater support. 'Politicians don't realise what communal spirit they could create by investing more heavily in music.'

One of Kuznetsov's admirers wonders whether he is in danger of not hanging onto 'the fearlessness of youth'. On the evidence of Kuznetsov's boldly assured new interpretation of the Brahms Concerto, which he plays on a new CD release, I'd say that his fearlessness is in no danger yet.

PAPER 2   WRITING (1 hour 30 minutes)

Part 1

You **must** answer this question. Write your answer in **180–220** words in an appropriate style.

---

1   You are the Secretary of the English Club at an international college. The club would like to see some improvements made to the English Language Library. The College Principal, Ms Roach, has asked you to write a proposal with recommendations for improvements to the library.

Read the information below about the library, on which you have made some notes. Then, **using the information appropriately**, write a proposal to Ms Roach outlining the current problems with the library, suggesting what changes you would like to make and explaining how these changes would benefit the students.

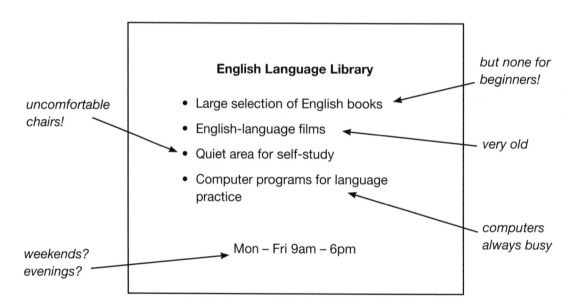

English Language Library

- Large selection of English books *but none for beginners!*
- English-language films *very old*
- Quiet area for self-study *uncomfortable chairs!*
- Computer programs for language practice *computers always busy*

Mon – Fri 9am – 6pm *weekends? evenings?*

Write your **proposal**. You should use your own words as far as possible.

Part 2

Write an answer to **one** of the questions (**2–5**) in this part. Write your answer in **220–260** words in an appropriate style.

---

2   You see this notice in an international magazine:

> ### Global Warming
>
> We are planning a special feature on how global warming affects different countries around the world. Write an article telling us how you think global warming is affecting your country and outlining ways in which people can deal with this problem.

Write your **article**.

3   In class you have been discussing communication. Your teacher has asked you to write an essay discussing the advantages and disadvantages of using computers as a way to communicate, giving reasons for your opinions.

Write your **essay**.

4   An Irish friend of yours is writing a book about working patterns around the world. She has asked you to write a contribution about work in your country. In your contribution, say whether people in your country remain in the same job for life or whether they tend to change jobs, giving reasons and explaining the effect this has on people's lifestyles.

Write your **contribution** to the book.

5   Answer one of the following two questions based on **one** of the titles below.

   (a) *Lord of the Flies* by William Golding

   You have been asked to write a review of *Lord of the Flies* for your college magazine. In your review, explain which of the characters you think is most interesting and why, and say whether you would recommend the story to other students.

   Write your **review**.

   (b) *The Lighthouse* by P D James

   In class, you have been discussing the importance of places in *The Lighthouse*. Your teacher has asked you to write a report about one of the places, saying why it is important to the development of the story.

   Write your **report**.

PAPER 3   USE OF ENGLISH (1 hour)

Part 1

For questions **1–12**, read the text below and decide which answer (**A**, **B**, **C** or **D**) best fits each gap.
There is an example at the beginning (**0**).
Mark your answers **on the separate answer sheet**.

Example:

0 A acceptance   **B** welcome   **C** entertainment   **D** admission

0	A	B	C	D

Jacqueline Wilson – children's novelist

Jacqueline Wilson has written dozens of novels, nearly all of them for children, and her fans give her a rock-star **(0)** .... whenever she visits a bookshop to sign copies of her books.

Her success as a novelist has been **(1)** .... on often painful stories about young teenagers, which are written with humour and a strong **(2)** .... that children are smart. Girls in particular adore her books because she **(3)** .... all their feelings, even the bad ones, about being teenagers, without ever moralising. But, perhaps because of her disturbing subject **(4)** .... , she often meets resistance from adults. Unlike some of her peers, she does not have a **(5)** .... among adults. It's all the more **(6)** .... , therefore, that sales of her books have **(7)** .... 20 million.

The book that finally made her **(8)** .... , after years as a little-known writer, was *The Story of Tracy Beaker*, published in 1991. It was quickly **(9)** .... by a TV company and is now a popular series. This **(10)** .... for Jacqueline Wilson came when she **(11)** .... with illustrator Nick Sharratt for the first time, and he played an important role in defining a 'look' for all her **(12)** .... novels. This 'look' reflects a flair for being childlike without being childish, and Jacqueline Wilson's winning formula continues to delight her readers.

1   **A**   built   **B**   formed   **C**   assembled   **D**   compiled

2   **A**   persuasion   **B**   opinion   **C**   conviction   **D**   sincerity

3   **A**   advocates   **B**   legitimises   **C**   credits   **D**   grants

4   **A**   theme   **B**   topic   **C**   meaning   **D**   matter

5   **A**   backing   **B**   favour   **C**   following   **D**   status

6   **A**   memorable   **B**   remarkable   **C**   noticeable   **D**   considerable

7   **A**   mounted   **B**   gained   **C**   topped   **D**   headed

8   **A**   celebrity   **B**   title   **C**   respect   **D**   name

9   **A**   fixed on   **B**   taken up   **C**   marked down   **D**   seen through

10   **A**   headway   **B**   progress   **C**   breakthrough   **D**   advance

11   **A**   mixed together   **B**   made up   **C**   teamed up   **D**   fitted together

12   **A**   subsequent   **B**   arising   **C**   consecutive   **D**   resulting

Part 2

For questions **13–27**, read the text below and think of the word which best fits each gap. Use only **one** word in each gap. There is an example at the beginning **(0)**.

Write your answers **IN CAPITAL LETTERS on the separate answer sheet**.

Example: `0` | `I` `S` | | | | | | | | | | | | | | | | |

Why do people do dangerous sports?

Psychologists say the desire to experience danger **(0)** …….. normal and healthy, imprinted by the lifestyle of our prehistoric ancestors. **(13)** …….. to a researcher at Sheffield University, when we faced real dangers almost daily **(14)** …….. satisfy the basic needs of hunger and thirst, there were challenges which required **(15)** …….. to stretch ourselves or we would not have survived.

Although now we live in a world that is far **(16)** …….. advanced, we feel compelled to seek new challenges in **(17)** …….. to feel good about ourselves. But the impulse to take risks varies markedly among individuals. It has to do **(18)** …….. the fact that some people are both biologically and psychologically endowed with a constitution that leads **(19)** …….. to seek very high levels of stimulation and excitement.

High-sensation seekers invariably set **(20)** …….. for exotic holiday locations, try foreign foods and enjoy heavy rock music or horror movies. It is believed that many people engage in hazardous activities to compensate for their humdrum lives, and will readily consider taking a short-term risk, **(21)** …….. as a bungee-jump. **(22)** …….. gives a positive buzz, adrenaline is released and you have the feeling that you've cheated death. But you wouldn't bungee-jump hour **(23)** …….. hour. Extreme risk-takers say they experience **(24)** …….. certain after-glow of euphoria that lasts for days, especially when they have had to overcome **(25)** …….. own fears. The result is a kind of amnesia: they forget all **(26)** …….. unpleasantness of the experience and cannot wait to repeat it. The effect can change people's lives **(27)** …….. good.

Visual materials for the Speaking test

- How effective might these ways of learning be?
- What difficulties might the students be experiencing?

- What do you think the people might be talking about?
- How important might their friendship with each other be?

- Why might these things be important for a good life?
- Which one would bring the greatest long-term satisfaction?

- What aspects of city life do the pictures show?
- How might the people be feeling?

- Why might the people be writing in these situations?
- How important is it for the people to write accurately?

- How successful might these activities be in encouraging young people to find out more about science?
- Which one would teach them the most?

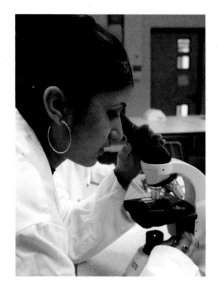

- Why do people organise events like these?
- What might the atmosphere at the events be like?

- What might motivate the people to do these things?
- How difficult might it be for the people to achieve success?

- What might children gain from these different experiences?
- Which two might be the most useful for the children in their adult lives?

- What might the people be learning by getting close to nature in these ways?
- How might the people be feeling?

- What would students learn from doing these activities after school?
- How popular might they be with students?

- What positive and negative effects have these types of technology had on people's lives?
- Which type of technology might bring the greatest benefit to people in the future?

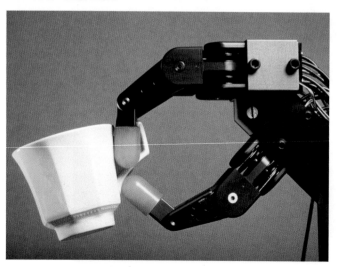

Part 3

For questions **28–37**, read the text below. Use the word given in capitals at the end of some of the lines to form a word that fits in the gap **in the same line**. There is an example at the beginning (**0**).

Write your answers **IN CAPITAL LETTERS on the separate answer sheet**.

Example:

| 0 | M | E | E | T | I | N | G | | | | | | | | | | | |

Polar travel

The Scott Polar Research Institute (SPRI) was established in 1920 as a

(**0**) ………..……... place for polar explorers and researchers. It is named after   **MEET**

Captain Scott, the leader of the legendary and ill-fated expedition to the

South Pole that took place between 1910 and 1913.

Scott recognised the importance of the new medium of photography for

purposes of generating (**28**) ……….……... and appointed a professional   **PUBLIC**

photographer to accompany his voyage to those icy and inhospitable regions.

This photographer's (**29**) ……….……... images of the expedition form a   **ATMOSPHERE**

(**30**) ………..……... part of the Institute's collection of archive material, and   **SIGNIFY**

remind us of the (**31**) ……….……... demanded of the early polar explorers.   **HERO**

In the past, while some polar expeditions were (**32**) ……….……... scientific,   **TRUE**

others were driven by pure (**33**) ……….……... instinct. Nowadays,   **COMPETE**

the principal reason for setting foot at the poles is scientific research.

Ice and air are very precise indicators of levels of climate change,

which is why, during coffee breaks at the Scott Polar Research

Institute today, the (**34**) ………..……... is that you will find groups of   **LIKELY**

(**35**) ……….……... , rather than explorers, exchanging ideas. Everyone   **ACADEMY**

admires those (**36**) ……….……... early pioneers, but today the main   **COURAGE**

purpose of travel to those frozen, (**37**) ……….……... regions, the last   **SPOIL**

wilderness on Earth, is environmental science.

Part 4

For questions **38–42**, think of **one** word only which can be used appropriately in all three sentences. Here is an example (**0**).

Example:

0 They say the new minister is a lovely person and very .... to talk to.

My neighbours have not had a very .... life, but they always seem cheerful.

It's .... enough to see why the town is popular with tourists.

Example:

0	E	A	S	Y														

Write **only** the missing word **IN CAPITAL LETTERS on the separate answer sheet**.

---

38 The tribesman used the .... edge of a stone to cut through the thick rope.

Be careful when you drive over the bridge because there's a .... bend on the other side.

Mario has a .... business brain and is bound to do well in the world of finance.

39 The experts reckon that the new Minister for Employment will be someone from the moderate .... of the party.

I had a window seat but I was right next to a .... so I couldn't see much as we flew over the mountains.

The hospital is pleased to announce that plans to build a new .... for accommodation for nurses have been approved.

40 The .... of the conflict are to be found in the events of the previous decade.

It was almost impossible to dig up all the .... of the old apple trees.

People in many parts of the world are now cut off from their peasant .... due to mass migration to cities.

41 There is a danger of explosion if .... is allowed to build up inside the cylinder.

Something needs to be done to reduce the .... imposed by management on members of staff as it is affecting their performance.

After breaking her ankle, Karen was warned by the doctor not to put any ....
on it.

42 The road was clear, and the speedometer .... 140 kph as the driver put his foot down hard on the accelerator.

It only .... me much later, when we were safely back on the beach, just how serious the situation had been when the boat overturned.

Alison stood up suddenly and .... her head hard on the low shelf behind her chair.

Part 5

For questions **43–50**, complete the second sentence so that it has a similar meaning to the first sentence, using the word given. **Do not change the word given**. You must use between **three** and **six** words, including the word given. Here is an example (**0**).

Example:

0 James would only speak to the head of department alone.

ON

James .... to the head of department alone.

The gap can be filled with the words 'insisted on speaking', so you write:

Example:	**0**	INSISTED ON SPEAKING

Write **only** the missing words **IN CAPITAL LETTERS on the separate answer sheet**.

---

43 It was several decades ago that a man first walked on the moon.

SINCE

It .... a man first walked on the moon.

44 The guide says that it will take us exactly two weeks to cross the desert.

CROSSED

The guide says that we .... exactly two weeks.

45 Could Ella have forgotten her bag today?

WONDER

I .... her bag behind today.

46 Some trees have been cut down, and as a result our garden is no longer private.

LOSS

Cutting down some trees has .... in our garden.

47 It was wrong to make Jean responsible for showing visitors round the building yesterday on her first day at work.

CHARGE

Jean should .... of showing visitors round the building yesterday on her first day at work.

48 Nick's cooking soon impressed his friends.

REPUTATION

Among his friends, Nick soon gained .... a good cook.

49 Someone has suggested changing the company logo.

FORWARD

A suggestion has .... the company logo.

50 Friends often remark on how much Clara resembles her sister.

TAKES

Friends often remark on the extent to .... her sister.

PAPER 4   LISTENING (approximately 40 minutes)

Part 1

You will hear three different extracts. For questions **1–6**, choose the answer (**A**, **B** or **C**) which fits best according to what you hear. There are two questions for each extract.

Extract One

You hear part of a radio programme about an ancient factory in the south of Spain.

1   The woman says that, in the past, the factory's main product

    A   gave off a powerful smell.

    B   was popular with poor people.

    C   had little commercial success.

2   Listeners to the programme who want to visit the site are advised to

    A   take the public bus service.

    B   walk along the coastal route.

    C   hire a car.

Extract Two

You hear a conversation between two inventors who have each made a lot of money.

3   They agree that a successful person is someone who has

    A   an optimistic attitude to life and work.

    B   a strong determination to beat all rivals.

    C   the skill to achieve a good standard of living from their business.

4   What gives the woman the drive to carry out unconventional projects?

    A   the need to prove to herself that she has retained her creativity

    B   the conviction that the most worthwhile ventures are risky

    C   the fact that people around her doubt her business methods

Extract Three

You hear two students discussing a talk they have been to about mushrooms and other fungi.

5   What is the aim of the project they heard about?

   A to protect endangered species of fungus

   B to record all species of fungus in one locality

   C to consolidate the findings of research on fungi

6   In the man's opinion, what is threatening the project?

   A a shortage of experts

   B a lack of interest among the public

   C the loss of woodland to urban development

Part 2

You will hear a woman called Emma Karlsson introducing a programme about a very old house she has visited in the countryside. For questions **7–14**, complete the sentences.

A house in the countryside

Emma uses the term

| | 7 | to describe the form the rest of the programme will take.

The programme concentrates on the | | 8 | of the building.

The oldest part of the present house was constructed in the

| | 9 | century.

The material the builder used for the walls was

| | 10 | mixed with plaster.

The owner of the house is currently a | | 11 | by profession.

Emma suggests that | | 12 | have lived in the house since it was built.

The noises you hear when the weather changes come from the

| | 13 | in the house's wooden frame.

Emma says that the noise made by the

| | 14 | in the building sounds like orchestral music.

Part 3

You will hear part of an interview in which a jazz musician and radio presenter called Harry Bulford is talking about his life and work. For questions **15–20**, choose the answer (**A, B, C** or **D**) which fits best according to what you hear.

---

15   What first attracted Harry to jazz?

    A an understanding of its emotional appeal
    B being told that he had a talent for it
    C his brother's enthusiasm for it
    D seeing it performed well

16   Harry says he went to music college because he wanted to

    A become a composer.
    B have a break from jazz.
    C fulfil his father's expectations.
    D show his contempt for conformity.

17   In his response to the question about whether he's 'Britain's top trumpeter', Harry reveals that he is

    A proud to be praised so highly.
    B keen to improve his skills even further.
    C embarrassed on behalf of other players.
    D resigned to being unknown internationally.

18   What does Harry enjoy about touring with his band?

    A having contact with his fans
    B working with fellow-musicians
    C the challenge of the tough schedule
    D the chance to be creative in his music

19   For Harry, one disadvantage of being a professional performer is that

    A his social circle tends to be limited.
    B he's been unable to protect his personal privacy.
    C he's had problems caused by a fluctuating income.
    D his frequent absences from home have affected his family life.

20   Harry thinks he was asked to present his current programme because

    A no one else was available at the time.
    B the producer was a former schoolfriend.
    C he was considered to have the right approach.
    D his previous programme had made him popular.

Part 4

You will hear five short extracts in which people are talking about major changes in their lives.

TASK ONE

For questions **21–25**, choose from the list (**A–H**) each speaker's main reason for changing their life.

TASK TWO

For questions **26–30**, choose from the list (**A–H**) the feeling each speaker has about their new way of life.

While you listen you must complete both tasks.

TASK ONE		TASK TWO	
A A new-found interest inspired me.	Speaker 1 **21**	**A** I'm a more confident person.	Speaker 1 **26**
B A close friend encouraged me.	Speaker 2 **22**	**B** I value the recognition I receive.	Speaker 2 **27**
C A lifelong hobby became the focus of my life.	Speaker 3 **23**	**C** I put more value on relationships.	Speaker 3 **28**
D An unexpected opportunity was offered to me.	Speaker 4 **24**	**D** I no longer depend on my family.	Speaker 4 **29**
E A shared family interest motivated me.	Speaker 5 **25**	**E** I'm glad to avoid a monotonous routine.	Speaker 5 **30**
F A good business opportunity tempted me.		**F** I feel I've given something back to society.	
G A bad experience on holiday changed my attitude.		**G** I thrive in a healthier environment.	
H A sudden problem prompted my decision.		**H** I'm more secure financially.	

PAPER 5   SPEAKING (15 minutes)

There are two examiners. One (the interlocutor) conducts the test, providing you with the necessary materials and explaining what you have to do. The other examiner (the assessor) is introduced to you, but then takes no further part in the interaction.

Part 1 (3 minutes)

The interlocutor first asks you and your partner a few questions. The interlocutor asks candidates for some information about themselves, then widens the scope of the questions by asking about e.g. candidates' leisure activities, studies, travel and daily life. Candidates are expected to respond to the interlocutor's questions and listen to what their partner has to say.

Part 2 (a one-minute 'long turn' for each candidate, plus a 30-second response from the second candidate)

You are each given the opportunity to talk for about a minute, and to comment briefly after your partner has spoken.

The interlocutor gives you a set of pictures and asks you to talk about them for about one minute. It is important to listen carefully to the interlocutor's instructions. The interlocutor then asks your partner a question about your pictures and your partner responds briefly.

You are then given another set of pictures to look at. Your partner talks about these pictures for about one minute. This time the interlocutor asks you a question about your partner's pictures and you respond briefly.

Part 3 (approximately 4 minutes)

In this part of the test, you and your partner are asked to talk together. The interlocutor places a new set of pictures on the table between you. This stimulus provides the basis for a discussion. The interlocutor explains what you have to do.

Part 4 (approximately 4 minutes)

The interlocutor asks some further questions, which leads to a more general discussion of what you have talked about in Part 3. You may comment on your partner's answers if you wish.

Test 4

PAPER 1 READING (1 hour 15 minutes)

Part 1

You are going to read three extracts which are all concerned in some way with family. For questions **1–6**, choose the answer (**A**, **B**, **C** or **D**) which you think fits best according to the text. Mark your answers **on the separate answer sheet**.

Extract from a novel

Summer in Italy

The summer I turned fifteen my father took me to the libraries of Rome to help him with his research. We were sharing a studio apartment with two rollaway beds and a prehistoric stereo system, and each morning for five weeks he chose a new classical masterpiece from the compilations he bought. He then woke me to the sound of violins and harpsichords at exactly half-past seven, reminding me that research waited for no man.

I would rise to find him shaving over the sink, or ironing his shirts, or counting the notes in his wallet, always humming along with the recording. Short as he was, he tended to every inch of his appearance, plucking strands of grey from his thick brown hair the way florists cull limp petals from roses. There was an internal vitality he was trying to preserve, a vivaciousness he thought was diminished by the crow's feet at the corners of his eyes, by the thinking man's wrinkles across his forehead. Whenever my imagination was dulled by the endless shelves of books where we spent our days, he was always quick to sympathise. So at lunchtime we would take to the streets for fresh pastries and ice cream and every evening he would bring me into town for sightseeing. One night he led me on a tour of the city's fountains, telling me to toss a lucky penny into each one.

1   What do we find out about the way the narrator's father looked?

   A   He tried hard to look like a mature academic.
   B   He had lines on his face caused by intense concentration.
   C   He looked younger than most men of his generation.
   D   He regularly dyed his hair.

2   What do we learn about the relationship between the narrator and his father?

   A   His father regarded the narrator as being young for his age.
   B   His father insisted that the narrator should enjoy research.
   C   His father recognised the narrator's need for relaxation.
   D   His father expected the narrator to make some decisions about their routine.

Extract from an autobiography

My aunt's wedding

When I was three, my mother made me a dress in cream silk for Aunt Ada's wedding. I was paraded and much admired. I relished the attention.

At the actual wedding, the bride naturally took over as the centre of everyone's approval, and I went off to join my boy cousins in a rip-roaring exploration of my surroundings. In one corner of the hall were stacks of wooden chairs piled high. This was just the place to hide. Without hesitation I was on my knees, scuttling within the network of chair legs. The forest darkened the further in I went, and the excitement subsided, giving way to panic. I began to cry. The cry was traced, the mountain of chairs dismantled, and I was snatched to bright lights and retribution. The dress was ruined, and my mother's rage, deflected in public behind tense laughter, was choked back and reserved for the reckoning to come. While my cousins were still running and chasing and having fun, I was led away, bewildered. Why were girls so different from boys?

Do I really remember all this for myself? I was only three, after all. And yet some indisputable objects remained to remind me – photographs, and the dress, demoted to doll's clothing. Perhaps I am reading more into it now I've grown older. Who is to say? What matters is that the story has become a family legend, evidence of what they saw to be my true nature – 'adventurous spirit' or 'cheeky rascal' – depending on who was making the assessment.

3   How did the writer feel after she was rescued from under the chairs?

    A   surprised that her mother was angry with her
    B   confused by an expected code of behaviour
    C   ashamed about being reprimanded in public
    D   upset that her hiding place had been discovered

4   In the third paragraph, what does the writer suggest about the incident?

    A   It has taught her some valuable lessons.
    B   Her family have misinterpreted its significance.
    C   It may have gained importance to her over time.
    D   She has almost certainly recalled it inaccurately.

How mothers and adult children communicate:
a psychologist's view

When children are small, every aspect of their lives is their mother's business. When they're grown, a mother may want to maintain that closeness by staying involved in their lives. But a grown-up daughter or son may overreact to what they hear as their mother's criticism, because they still see their mother as all-powerful. Adult children often don't realise the power they have, and don't realise that mothers continue to offer advice or help because they know they are powerless – they are not needed any more. When an adult son accuses his mother of criticising, the mother sincerely denies this. And when the mother says she wasn't criticising, the son rejects this because he knows he feels criticised. Any remark meant to offer advice, suggestions or help implies criticism, but it also shows caring by paying attention to details of your life and appearance at a level that normally only you yourself would pay. Here's an example. A young woman showed her mother a new purchase: two pairs of socks – one black, one dark navy blue. The next day her mother asked, 'Are you sure you're not wearing one of each colour?' The woman told me, 'That's just the sort of thing that would have infuriated me in the past. I'd have thought, "What kind of incompetent do you think I am?"' But, remembering what she'd read of my analysis, she reminded herself, 'Who else would care about the colour of my socks?' With that, her anger dissipated.

5   What does the writer say about the balance of power between mothers and their grown-up children?

   A   Children use it to their advantage.
   B   It is misunderstood by both parties.
   C   Both parties often attempt to change it.
   D   Mothers are more aware of how it has shifted.

6   The writer gives the example of the socks to illustrate the need for

   A   children to appreciate the motivation behind a perceived insult.
   B   children to follow their mothers' advice, however critical it seems.
   C   mothers to demonstrate more concern for their children.
   D   mothers to make comments in a non-offensive manner.

Part 2

You are going to read an extract from a novel. Six paragraphs have been removed from the extract. Choose from the paragraphs **A–G** the one which fits each gap (**7–12**). There is one extra paragraph which you do not need to use.

Mark your answers **on the separate answer sheet.**

Chance encounter

I ease behind a slender tree trunk, then hold an opened palm toward my dog Keta. In our silent language it means 'lie down and stay'. She obeys. A few minutes later the deer steps into plain sight, and leans down to graze, nuzzling back and forth amid the lush grass. So exquisite is she that it takes a supreme act of self-control to keep myself from jumping up and shouting aloud.

7	

I turn to look into Keta's eyes. Firmly now, I point to a low spot behind the little hillock where we stand. She folds back her ears and walks away, stopping several times to face me, sad-eyed and pleading, but obedient. When I give the signal, she lies down. I start toward the deer, always closely watching to be sure she's busy feeding, so the sound of her picking and chewing will mask the unavoidable crunch of my bootsteps.

8	

Perhaps it's because I haven't brought a rifle, not even for protection against stumbling into a bear. I've come here to hunt only with my eyes, and to marvel at this graceful creature. I wonder if hawks and herons, wolves and killer whales are ever astounded by the loveliness, grace and perfection of their prey.

9	

I turn from her gaze and view the landscape it encompasses: the green tangle at her feet; the forest that shelters her from rain, wind and snow; the dense thickets that shade and conceal her; the nearby shore, where kelp left by winter storms sustains her through the lean months; and the tundra heights where she finds seclusion in the long summer days.

10	

I know immediately that Keta must have forgotten her instructions or chosen to ignore them. Sure enough, she's on the move: she's zigzagging excitedly, weaving herself through streamers of scent, still trying to spot the deer beyond the pines. The deer breaks into a stylized mechanical strut, heading up the slope toward a scatter of trees and underbrush. There's nothing to lose, so I imitate the soft, sheeplike bleat of a young deer.

11	

The call keeps her from dashing off but can't ease her alarm. She moves slowly and silently. She looks at us repeatedly, but seems less trusting of her eyes than of the telling evidence a different sense will give her. I know exactly what she's trying to do and vainly wish for a way to change it.

12	

For a brief moment I had felt that we were more alike than different, and that I had known and understood her. But in the vast quiet she leaves behind, I am quite overwhelmed by the sense of distance between our two worlds.

A   But now, looking back at the deer, I find that something has gone awry. She's standing in a rigid pose: head raised, ears wide, body tense. What could have frightened her, since I haven't moved, haven't given a hint of my presence? Then I realise she isn't looking at me at all, but past me, and I hear a shuffle in the grass.

B   But like Keta, I hold a tenuous grip on myself, standing still in the warm breeze, holding my binoculars to my eyes. The deer is unaware of us, contentedly plucking at the undergrowth. Her eyes move this way and that as she feeds, revealing the white crescents at their edges.

C   Keta's behaviour telegraphs the scent's increasing strength: she moves forward, catches herself and looks back, like someone pacing at a line she's been warned not to cross. She probes her nose into the breeze, occasionally reaching to the side for a stronger ribbon of scent.

D   As if in answer to my question, she lifts her elegant head and looks toward me. I stare back through my binoculars. Her globed eyes stand out from her face so she can look forward along her snout. The morning sky reflects on their dark surface the way clouds shimmer on still water.

E   She stops immediately … then turns and steps deliberately back toward us, as if I were pulling a line attached to her neck. She's caught by an insuppressible curiosity, yet I can almost feel the quavering intensity of her fear.

F   She lifts her snout into the air, and picks up our scent. With utmost dignity she raises one foreleg and slowly turns aside. Then she bounds to the crest of the slope, springs over a fallen log, and vanishes into the forest, as if on a cloud of her own breath.

G   I know myself as a predator. And considering how I've stalked this animal – slipped through the boundaries of her solitude, hidden my shape, and used the wind to conceal my footsteps – I wonder that I can feel so innocent.

Part 3

You are going to read a newspaper article. For questions **13–19**, choose the answer (**A**, **B**, **C** or **D**) which you think fits best according to the text.
Mark your answers **on the separate answer sheet**.

Red Shift
Jake Willis meets Scottish band Red Shift and considers their new album.

I'm waiting in a stylish photography studio in North London. The walk here wasn't too promising: a few factories, a couple of goods yards with barbed wire along the top of the walls, a grimy concrete shopping mall. Inside though, it's exclusive and plush. And I'm inclined to describe the contrast between the world out there and the world in here, since the band I'm about to interview would seem to have a foot in both camps. If their songs are to be taken at face value, they might be perceived as a bunch of scruffy kids who spend their time hanging around on rainy street corners, bored and penniless. And if the newspapers are to be believed, they're now millionaire rock stars with glamorous girlfriends and celebrity show-business chums.

On the stroke of 11 a.m., Red Shift arrive. The four of them are prompt, polite, happy, clean – my immediate impression is how, well, nice they seem, with something approaching a 'boyband' sheen about them. Their manager, Dave Maxwell, is wearing a polo shirt and trainers, and taken in combination with the white back wall of the studio, they could easily be a set of lads who have just arrived with someone's dad for a game of squash.

The 'legend' of Red Shift runs something like this. Four schoolmates get musical instruments for birthday presents and start rehearsing in a garage. Next minute they're a phenomenon; releasing two number one singles and a blockbuster first album, winning a clutch of awards and headlining top music festivals. Somewhere along the line, they're also credited with rewriting the music business rulebook, having foregone airplay and marketing, and manifested themselves virally through websites and online file-sharing. 'Er no, not really,' says lead singer and songwriter Ben Gardner, once the photo shoot is over and we sit down to coffee. 'We really didn't know anything about that stuff. It wasn't a plan. It just happened.' Take it or leave it nonchalance among the successful is often a hindsight re-branding of desperation, but in the case of Red Shift, I'm inclined to believe them.

We finish our coffee, and I ask Gardner about his lyrics, and in particular the number of allusions to 1970s/early 80s popular culture he makes. 'It's just humour,' he explains. 'I love all that "retro" stuff, and try and get in as many references as I can.' And whether he appreciates it or not, humour is one of the things that elevates him above most of his contemporaries. Like so many estimable British lyricists before him, Gardner has always been willing to risk a delightful irony or witty turn of phrase, even in a sad song, while most of his contemporaries are content to juggle clichés or trot out vacuous abstractions.

In conversation Gardner comes over as reticent, and at times almost embarrassed by his own success – as if being an ordinary kid from a dull working-class Scottish town and an award-winning singer-songwriter were somehow completely incongruous. Maybe it's only since moving to New York that he finally feels at home with who and what he is. Pushing a bit harder, I ask him if he worries that he's now living thousands of miles from all the things that have provided the sources for his songwriting so far, including his dialect and his friends. He simply shrugs his shoulders, saying, 'There are other things to write about.'

So we move on to their new album *Downtime*, due for release at the end of the week. I already adore it. However, as Gardner once famously pointed out, love is not only blind but deaf, and I can imagine that less besotted listeners may find it a more challenging proposition. There are no anthems as such, the kind of thing that the bulk of Red Shift's followers like to chant along to at concerts, and no obvious chart-toppers.

Downtime was produced in California, and with its booming guitars and reverberating bass lines, the album's 'stateside' influence is clear. And there's more of that upbeat country and western sound that first came to light on Gardner's recent album recorded with US band Rebound. This makes me wonder if Gardner is not only cracking the whip but holding the reins as well now, steering the band in his own favoured direction.

Will the album please the music critics? Well, that remains to be seen. The proof of the pudding, as they say, is in the eating. But for the band members themselves, no such quality-control test is necessary. In fact, four more likeable and well-adjusted young men you are unlikely to meet. I might even throw the word 'modest' in their direction, and in some cases, even shy. However meteoric their rise, they appear to have their feet well and truly planted on planet Earth. In an industry that prides itself on excess and promotes itself through legends of extravagance, perhaps this isn't something *line 95* that Red Shift's management or even the band themselves want to hear, but I speak as I find.

13 The writer describes the studio and its surroundings in order to

    A stress the contrast between the location and the band.
    B highlight certain conflicting images of the band.
    C discredit certain myths surrounding the band.
    D illustrate his mixed feelings about the band.

14 The writer makes a favourable distinction between Red Shift and bands who

    A deny accusations about their early years.
    B claim to have planned out their musical careers.
    C pretend to have been surprised by their achievements.
    D lie about their motives for entering the music business.

15 What does the writer say about Ben Gardner?

    A He brings a variety of emotions to his lyrics.
    B He is unaware of how talented a songwriter he is.
    C He pays tribute to the style of certain British lyricists.
    D He takes more chances with his lyrics than other songwriters do.

16 What does Ben Gardner suggest about his lifestyle in the fifth paragraph?

    A He is unsure whether being a successful singer-songwriter is compatible with having modest origins.
    B He is unconcerned about being cut off from the original inspiration for his songs.
    C He feels that it's taken him some time to get used to living in New York.
    D He admits that he misses certain aspects of his life in Scotland.

17 In the writer's opinion, Red Shift's new album *Downtime* may

    A consolidate their status as musicians.
    B disappoint some of their more devoted fans.
    C attract a different audience from previous albums.
    D have a more limited appeal than previous albums.

18 What does the writer suggest about the sound of the new album?

    A It has influenced the musical style of other bands.
    B It does not do justice to the skills of the band members.
    C It is not necessarily the chosen style of all the band members.
    D It indicates a change of leadership among the band members.

19 The word 'this' in line 95 refers to the writer's view of

    A the band members' personalities.
    B the band's prospects of success.
    C the band members' musical talent.
    D the band's reputation in the industry.

Part 4

You are going to read a magazine article about technology and sport. For questions **20–34**, choose from the sections (**A–D**). The sections may be chosen more than once.
Mark your answers **on the separate answer sheet**.

Which section mentions the following?

equipment designed to function less powerfully than previously	**20**
a product designed to monitor performance	**21**
a choice of design available for particular weather conditions	**22**
a piece of equipment designed to have a short lifespan	**23**
a response to an improvement in performance in a sport	**24**
portable technology to assist in training	**25**
a sport demanding a degree of courage as well as skill	**26**
totally rethinking a sports product	**27**
performance benefiting from a relatively small financial outlay	**28**
the eventual adaptation of equipment to suit each athlete's particular needs	**29**
using observation of the body's natural movement to drive design	**30**
the need for experience when using high-tech equipment	**31**
making a sport less dangerous	**32**
athletes expressing dissatisfaction with the existing technology	**33**
reducing the weight and bulk of a sports product	**34**

ENGINEERING IN SPORT

Technology now plays a vital part across a range of sports. Matthew King looks at the state of play.

A

In a sport where technique, individual strength and teamwork all come into play, how can a coach tell if one of the eight men in a boat isn't pulling his weight? Two mechanical engineering students have designed a strain gauge that fits onto the blade of the oar and, by showing how much it bends, reveals how hard a rower is working. The usual way to test a rower's strength is in the gym, but they wanted to measure it in the water. The prototype gauge weighs about 300g and attaches to the front of the blade, securely enough to give accurate readings but still easy to take on and off. It sends readings to a cigar-box-sized data-logger in the boat and the information can then be downloaded onto a laptop. Back on land, the coach can check, on clear graphical read-outs, whether everybody is in synch, and can analyse every stroke made. This can later translate into a more efficient, powerful stroke. The good news is that the whole system ought to be well within the budget of every boat club.

B

Redesigning the running shoe may seem as daunting and futile an engineering assignment as reinventing the wheel. But freelance designer Mark MacKenzie saw there is always room for improvement. Liaising with two serious runners and studying in detail what actually happens when you run, he made two crucial breakthroughs: firstly, that running barefoot is ergonomically healthier; it alters the physical forces at work, and provides better exercise. Secondly, that elite sprinters run entirely on their toes for the first 80m of a 100m race. MacKenzie developed a shoe to mimic the natural running action of the naked foot. 'I've got rid of the heel completely, making the shoe more compact and also much lighter. This forces the runner on to their toes, which is faster and healthier,' he says. His top-specification spike, for elite athletes, is so light it would only be strong enough to be worn two or three times. However, MacKenzie is also looking at the mass market. He has incorporated some of the features of the original into a leisure trainer for longer-distance runners.

C

Making things that work at maximum efficiency is one of engineering's goals. But javelins are designed to underperform for one very good reason. By the 1980s, competition standards had risen so much that athletes routinely recorded throws of over 90m, culminating in a 104.8m throw. Officials recognised that it was only a matter of time before a javelin would land among spectators, with potentially lethal results. The solution, introduced in 1986, was elegant in its simplicity: the centre of balance of javelins was moved forward 4cm. They now fly in a more pronounced arc, travel about 20m less and usually land point first. Top athletes use javelins made of either aluminium or carbon-fibre, weighing about 800g, with a narrower point for headwinds and a wider one for tailwinds. The range of their throws is now more consistent. Even if technology isn't allowed to improve the javelin, it can improve technique.

D

Pole vaulting is the most technical of all track and field events. It takes strength, co-ordination and nerves of steel to run at full tilt with a long pole, plant it, use its spring to hoist yourself upwards feet first, then twist your body up and over a bar. In the 1960s, bamboo poles were widely felt to be inadequate by the top vaulters, and were duly superseded by glass-fibre ones. Carbon-fibre composite was then added to increase stiffness and reduce twisting in use. While a pole is bending during a jump, the greatest stresses on it are in the middle. So manufacturers vary the thickness of the internal walls of the pole, making them thicker in the middle and thinner at the ends. Carbon-fibre poles are not for beginners. They store more energy but recoil more quickly, making it more difficult to swing hard and fast enough to get on top of the bend. The take-off time is only 100ths of a second and if the pole begins to bend while the vaulter is still on the ground, all the energy is lost. Ways to control bending and stiffness are being investigated, as is the quality of manufacture. Ultimately, poles will be tailored to the individual competitor.

Test 4

PAPER 2   WRITING (1 hour 30 minutes)

Part 1

You **must** answer this question. Write your answer in **180–220** words in an appropriate style.

1   You are the secretary of the social club at an international college in Ireland. A social event is held annually to celebrate the end of the college year, and the college Principal, Dr Masters, has written to you about this.

Read the Principal's email below. Then, **using the information appropriately**, write a proposal addressed to the Principal describing which event you think would be best, explaining why you think it would be the most suitable event and suggesting how it could be organised.

From:	D.Masters@lsrn.org
Subject:	End of Year Celebration

Popular events in the past were:
- disco and barbecue in college
- visit to local theatre and meal in restaurant
- coach trip to Dublin – shopping/sightseeing

Which of these do you recommend for this year? Remember, the students don't have much money but will want something memorable. How could we organise it?

Let me have your ideas.

Dr Masters (Principal)

Write your **proposal**. You should use your own words as far as possible.

Part 2

Write an answer to **one** of the questions **2–5** in this part. Write your answer in **220–260** words in an appropriate style.

---

2   You see the following announcement in an international magazine.

> ### Computer Games
>
> We're going to be publishing a special edition on computer games. We'd like readers to submit articles on this topic. Send us an article explaining why people enjoy playing computer games, outlining what you can learn from playing them and suggesting what the disadvantages of playing computer games are.

Write your **article**.

3   In class, you have been discussing the rise in consumerism. Your teacher has asked you to write an essay saying if you agree with the following statement:

In today's consumer society, people place too much importance on things that cost a lot of money.

Write your **essay**.

4   You read the following announcement in an international magazine.

> ### Transport problems around the world
>
> We are doing some research into different transport problems around the world. We would like our readers to contribute to our research by answering the following questions:
> * What is the biggest problem with transport in your country?
> * What has caused this problem?
> * What possible solutions might there be?

Write your **contribution** to the research project.

5   Answer **one** of the following two questions based on **one** of the titles below.

   (a) *Through a Glass, Darkly* by Donna Leon

   You have been asked to recommend a story about the environment for your college library. You decide to recommend *Through a Glass, Darkly*. In your report, discuss how the topic of the environment is important in the story and say why you would recommend the story to others.

   Write your **report**.

   (b) *Of Mice and Men* by John Steinbeck

   You see the following announcement in *Arts Today*, an English language journal, and decide to write about the story *Of Mice and Men*.

   > We are exploring the theme of friendship in stories and would like to publish readers' articles about friendship in a story they know.

   In your article, you should describe what you believe the qualities of a good friend should be and explain to what extent the relationship between Lennie and George demonstrates these qualities.

   Write your **article**.

PAPER 3   USE OF ENGLISH (1 hour)

Part 1

For questions **1–12**, read the text below and decide which answer (**A**, **B**, **C** or **D**) best fits each gap. There is an example at the beginning (**0**).
Mark your answers **on the separate answer sheet**.

Example:

0 A passage   **B** voyage   **C** expedition   **D** trip

	A	B	C	D
0	☐	☐	☐	▬

The Orient Express

In 1867, a wealthy Belgian called Georges Nagelmackers took a long **(0)** .... across the United States in one of George Pullman's transcontinental trains with their rubber shock absorbers and luxurious compartments. Before the 1860s, train carriages were little more than boxes on wheels, in which passengers were **(1)** .... jolted around. The revolutionary Pullman sleepers meant that Americans could now travel from one side of their vast country to the other in **(2)** .... comfort.

Realising how **(3)** .... it would be to be able to travel across Europe in similar **(4)** .... , Nagelmackers spent the next decade **(5)** .... with the authorities to allow his own specially designed sleeper trains to cross European **(6)** ....

It was not until 1919 that Nagelmackers' dream of a fast, first-class service from Paris in the west to Constantinople in the east finally became **(7)** .... The Orient Express, as this train is called, immediately **(8)** .... the imagination of the public and became the subject of **(9)** .... tales and legends. Not just the fictional James Bond in *From Russia with Love*, but many real-life spies are known to have **(10)** .... out secret assignments on the train, and a **(11)** .... element in the plot of Agatha Christie's novel *Murder on the Orient Express* is based on an actual incident from 1929.

For half a century, the train flourished. As passenger flights gradually replaced rail travel, **(12)** .... , the Orient Express became increasingly uncompetitive and only a few carriages remain today.

1   **A**   painfully   **B**   harmfully   **C**   wrongfully   **D**   hurtfully

2   **A**   high   **B**   entire   **C**   total   **D**   major

3   **A**   fair   **B**   advantageous   **C**   accessible   **D**   suitable

4   **A**   custom   **B**   method   **C**   style   **D**   form

5   **A**   discussing   **B**   dealing   **C**   contracting   **D**   negotiating

6   **A**   borders   **B**   limits   **C**   lines   **D**   margins

7   **A**   practice   **B**   reality   **C**   truth   **D**   certainty

8   **A**   took   **B**   kept   **C**   pulled   **D**   caught

9   **A**   immeasurable   **B**   countless   **C**   immense   **D**   infinite

10 **A**   held   **B**   brought   **C**   carried   **D**   sent

11 **A**   compulsory   **B**   crucial   **C**   primary   **D**   necessary

12 **A**   nonetheless   **B**   however   **C**   moreover   **D**   additionally

Part 2

For questions **13–27**, read the text below and think of the word which best fits each gap. Use only **one** word in each gap. There is an example at the beginning (**0**).

Write your answers **IN CAPITAL LETTERS on the separate answer sheet**.

Example: | **0** | B | E | T | W | E | E | N | | | | | | | | | |

In pursuit of excellence

In the early 1990s, the psychologist K Anders Ericsson and two colleagues conducted some research into the relationship **(0)** …….. talent and hard work at Berlin's elite Academy of Music. The curious thing **(13)** …….. , they couldn't find any musicians who could excel without any effort, or who could get to the top without practising as much as all **(14)** …….. peers. Also, they were unable to find any people who worked harder than everyone else and yet just didn't have exactly **(15)** …….. it takes to break into the top ranks. So their research would certainly seem to indicate that once someone makes **(16)** …….. into a top music school, the thing that distinguishes one performer from **(17)** …….. is how hard he or she works. That's it. What's more, with the musicians right **(18)** …….. the very top, it's not just a case of their **(19)** …….. worked harder, they have worked much, much harder.

This idea **(20)** …….. excellence requiring a minimum level of practice, arises time **(21)** …….. time in studies of expertise in various fields. In fact, researchers have come **(22)** …….. an agreement on what they believe to be the number of hours of practice required **(23)** …….. true expertise: 10,000. In their research, they have yet to come across **(24)** …….. who has accomplished world-class expertise in less time. It seems that people need **(25)** …….. amount of time in order for them to take **(26)** …….. everything they need to know to achieve genuine mastery. This is true even with individuals we think of **(27)** …….. geniuses.

Part 3

For questions **28–37**, read the text below. Use the word given in capitals at the end of some of the lines to form a word that fits in the gap **in the same line**. There is an example at the beginning (**0**).

Write your answers **IN CAPITAL LETTERS on the separate answer sheet**.

Example: | 0 | N | E | T | W | O | R | K | | | | | | | | | |

The people of the Orinoco Delta

The Orinoco Delta is a vast **(0)** …….. of waterways weaving through a   **NET**

jungle which carries the **(28)** …….. waters of the River Orinoco to the   **MUD**

Atlantic Ocean. The delta has formed over thousands of years as the river

has deposited millions of tonnes of sediment into the ocean, creating

41,000 sq km of densely **(29)** …….. islands, swamps and lagoons.   **FOREST**

The   Warao,   **(30)** ……..   the   'Canoe   People',   are   the   native   **LITERAL**

(31) …….. of the delta. They constitute the second largest indigenous tribe   **INHABIT**

in Venezuela with a population of 24,000. Although they were forced to

(32) …….. to remoter areas of the jungle by major damming work in the   **LOCATE**

1960s, family groups still reside **(33)** …….. in wooden houses raised on   **PEACE**

stilts along the banks of the river, and spend most of their time either

fishing in **(34)** …….. waterways in canoes, or hunting and gathering in the   **NEAR**

(35) …….. forests.   **ROUND**

The Warao build their houses and canoes from forest wood using traditional

techniques and make **(36)** …….. and other jewellery, baskets and hammocks   **NECK**

from the leaves and seeds of the moriche palm. Otherwise known as the

'tree of life', the moriche provides the Warao with fruit, juices and sweet pulp

to make bread. Also, the trunk of the palm is used to cultivate a small worm,

which provides a **(37)** …….. nutritious supplement to their diet.   **RELATE**

Part 4

For questions **38–42**, think of **one** word only which can be used appropriately in all three sentences. Here is an example (**0**).

Example:

0 They say the new minister is a lovely person and very ……………….. to talk to.

My neighbours have not had a very ……………….. life, but they always seem cheerful.

It's ……………….. enough to see why the town is popular with tourists.

Example: | **0** | E | A | S | Y | | | | | | | | | | | | | | |

Write **only** the missing word **IN CAPITAL LETTERS on the separate answer sheet.**

---

38 The first ……………….. of the phone woke José up and he reached out to answer it.

During the solar eclipse, you could see an amazing ……………….. of bright light as the moon passed over the sun.

The police exposed a large smuggling ……………….. that had been in existence for several years.

39 The friends we were visiting lived right in the ……………….. of the old city.

Alan just didn't have the ……………….. to tell his wife that he didn't like her new dress.

The biology teacher told her students that, now they had studied the ……………….. , they would go on to examine the other organs of the body.

40 Lead is an unusual metal in that it is ……………….. enough to bend at ordinary temperatures, yet melts at comparatively low heat.

You're far too ……………….. with that dog – it needs to be dealt with more strictly.

This is my favourite sweater because it is very ……………….. and light, but also extremely warm.

41   My grandmother ……………….. on a small pension so she's always looking for bargains in the shops.

Alfonso's name is well known in his home town and, though he died 300 years ago, his reputation ……………….. on.

She is a strict vegetarian and ……………….. on a diet of carrots, cabbage and apples.

42   People said that the mayor had ……………….. an important role in bringing the Olympic Games to the city.

As a child, Joe often ……………….. with his food instead of eating it, which used to annoy his mother.

Can you remember which radio station ……………….. Mozart's music all day to celebrate his birthday?

Part 5

For questions **43–50**, complete the second sentence so that it has a similar meaning to the first sentence, using the word given. **Do not change the word given**. You must use between **three** and **six** words, including the word given. Here is an example (**0**).

Example:

0 James would only speak to the head of department alone.

ON

James .... to the head of department alone.

The gap can be filled with the words 'insisted on speaking', so you write:

Example: | **0** | INSISTED ON SPEAKING

Write **only** the missing words **IN CAPITAL LETTERS on the separate answer sheet**.

---

43 It was only at the start of the following week that Kate saw Mark again.

UNTIL

Kate .... the start of the following week.

44 We could do our homework and then go to the cinema.

GOING

Why don't .... to the cinema?

45 Museum exhibits are usually electronically protected so that no-one can steal them.

PREVENT

Museum exhibits are usually electronically protected to .... stolen.

46 Jim would do anything at all to help his brother.

NOT

There is absolutely .... to help his brother.

47 Richie was coming to dinner this evening but it seems he has decided not to.

CHANGED

Richie seems ………………………………… coming to dinner this evening.

48 When I eventually got through security, the departure gate was about to close.

TIME

The departure gate was on the point …………………………………..… I got through security.

49 Because of the problems with the buses that morning, all of the students came late to the lesson.

TURNED

Because of the problems with the buses that morning, not …………………………………..… to the lesson on time.

50 When it comes to sport, there is very little that Ann doesn't know.

GAPS

There are very …………………………………..… of sport.

PAPER 4 LISTENING (approximately 40 minutes)

Part 1

You will hear three different extracts. For questions **1–6**, choose the answer (**A, B** or **C**) which fits best according to what you hear. There are two questions for each extract.

Extract One

You hear two students discussing projects they have to do in the final year of their course.

1 What is the boy's idea for a project?

   A to write a short story

   B to make a movie

   C to compose a piece of music

2 What does the girl think of the boy's idea?

   A It sounds technically over-ambitious.

   B It could require outside help.

   C It might be too time-consuming.

Extract Two

You overhear a man telling a friend about an encounter with a bear during a recent trip to North America.

3 Why does he mention the end of his story almost immediately?

   A to show his involvement in the whole event

   B to highlight the most interesting part

   C to try and reassure his friend

4 What does his friend feel about the bear's adventure?

   A She'd have handled it all better if she'd been present.

   B The bear must have been completely unaffected.

   C Cars shouldn't be allowed through bear country.

Extract Three

You overhear two friends talking about buying books.

5   What do they disagree about?

   A   the value of personal recommendations

   B   the advantages of reading reviews

   C   the practicality of ordering online

6   What does the woman think of the café in her local bookshop?

   A   It's a waste of space that could be used for books.

   B   It's a useful way of getting to know like-minded people.

   C   It benefits customers as they can read books for free.

Part 2

You will hear a student called Guy Briggs giving a presentation at college about his experience of learning to surf. For questions **7–14**, complete the sentences.

Learning to surf

Guy says that his previous experience of

| | 7 | was helpful when learning to surf.

Guy recommends the local surf school called

| | 8 |, which he attended.

Guy hadn't realised that he'd have to wear a

| | 9 | on the surfing course.

Guy learnt about the importance of looking out for

| | 10 | on the beach when surfing.

Guy's instructor used the term

| | 11 | to describe the various features of the surfboard.

On the second day, Guy did some exercises to help his

| | 12 |, which had been painful.

On the fourth day, Guy learnt some new moves called

| | 13 |, which made the surfing more exciting.

On the final day, Guy's instructor said that

| | 14 | was important for avoiding injury.

Part 3

You will hear an interview with a singer-songwriter called Madeleine Marten, who is talking about her life and career. For questions **15–20**, choose the answer (**A**, **B**, **C** or **D**) which fits best according to what you hear.

15   Madeleine thinks her first hit single has remained popular because

    A   the singers who performed with her are now big stars.
    B   it has a particularly memorable accompanying video.
    C   it has a message people can still relate to.
    D   the music was ahead of its time.

16   What does Madeleine say about having to adopt a professional name?

    A   The disadvantages have outweighed the benefits.
    B   It met with some resistance from some people.
    C   It has taken her a long time to get used to it.
    D   The change continues to cause confusion.

17   How did having a part in a musical help Madeleine?

    A   It led to further offers of work on stage.
    B   It provided inspiration for her songwriting.
    C   It enabled her to make some useful contacts.
    D   It allowed her to re-establish a routine in her life.

18   Madeleine thinks that stars who seem to be behaving badly

    A   might just be expressing their creativity.
    B   may be unaware the public doesn't approve.
    C   may just be keen to get media exposure.
    D   might behave equally poorly in another profession.

19   Madeleine thinks that she hasn't become a big star because she

    A   is too honest to push her way to the top.
    B   has been too ready to listen to other people.
    C   has never had enough say in her own career.
    D   is quick to blame herself when things go wrong.

20   Compared to her earlier work, Madeleine thinks that her latest songs

    A   reflect her pop music roots more.
    B   reveal more about her as a person.
    C   have more carefully written lyrics.
    D   owe a greater debt to her producer.

Part 4

You will hear five short extracts in which people are talking about a change they are making in their lifestyles.

TASK ONE

For questions **21–25**, choose from the list (**A–H**) the lifestyle change each speaker is talking about.

TASK TWO

For questions **26–30**, choose from the list (**A–H**) each speaker's current feeling about their lifestyle change.

While you listen you must complete both tasks.

A retraining for a new career	**A** confused about their targets
B improving personal mobility	**B** unsure if they can maintain their efforts
C forming a group to perform with	**C** determined to prove someone wrong
D getting involved in voluntary work	**D** surprised by their family's reaction
E taking up an exercise programme	**E** pleased with their achievements so far
F growing and cooking organic vegetables	**F** dissatisfied with their rate of progress
G recycling waste material	**G** apologetic about needing praise
H using public transport more regularly	**H** aware of the financial implications

Speaker 1 **21**
Speaker 2 **22**
Speaker 3 **23**
Speaker 4 **24**
Speaker 5 **25**

Speaker 1 **26**
Speaker 2 **27**
Speaker 3 **28**
Speaker 4 **29**
Speaker 5 **30**

PAPER 5   SPEAKING (15 minutes)

There are two examiners. One (the interlocutor) conducts the test, providing you with the necessary materials and explaining what you have to do. The other examiner (the assessor) is introduced to you, but then takes no further part in the interaction.

Part 1 (3 minutes)

The interlocutor first asks you and your partner a few questions. The interlocutor asks candidates for some information about themselves, then widens the scope of the questions by asking about e.g. candidates' leisure activities, studies, travel and daily life. Candidates are expected to respond to the interlocutor's questions and listen to what their partner has to say.

Part 2 (a one-minute 'long turn' for each candidate, plus a 30-second response from the second candidate)

You are each given the opportunity to talk for about a minute, and to comment briefly after your partner has spoken.

The interlocutor gives you a set of pictures and asks you to talk about them for about one minute. It is important to listen carefully to the interlocutor's instructions. The interlocutor then asks your partner a question about your pictures and your partner responds briefly.

You are then given another set of pictures to look at. Your partner talks about these pictures for about one minute. This time the interlocutor asks you a question about your partner's pictures and you respond briefly.

Part 3 (approximately 4 minutes)

In this part of the test you and your partner are asked to talk together. The interlocutor places a new set of pictures on the table between you. This stimulus provides the basis for a discussion. The interlocutor explains what you have to do.

Part 4 (approximately 4 minutes)

The interlocutor asks some further questions, which leads to a more general discussion of what you have talked about in Part 3. You may comment on your partner's answers if you wish.

Paper 5 Frames

Test 1

Note: In the examination, there will be both an assessor and an interlocutor in the exam. The visual material for **Test 1** appears on pages C1 and C2 (Part 2), and C3 (Part 3).

Part 1   3 minutes (5 minutes for groups of three)

Interlocutor:	Good morning/afternoon/evening. My name is .... and this is my colleague ....

And your names are?

Can I have your mark sheets, please?

Thank you.

First of all we'd like to know something about you.

Select one or two questions and ask candidates in turn, as appropriate.

- Where are you from?
- What do you do here/there?
- How long have you been studying English?
- What do you enjoy most about learning English?

Select one or more questions from any of the following categories, as appropriate.

Surroundings

- Would you rather live in the countryside, or in a town or city? ...... (Why?)
- When you go to a restaurant, which is more important to you: the atmosphere or the food?

Hopes and ambitions

- Do you consider yourself to be an ambitious person? ...... (Why? / Why not?)
- What kind of job do you think would suit you best? ...... (Why?)

Part 2   4 minutes (6 minutes for groups of three)

People studying

Friendship

Interlocutor:	In this part of the test, I'm going to give each of you three pictures. I'd like you to talk about them on your own for about a minute, and also to answer a question briefly about your partner's pictures.
	(Candidate A), it's your turn first. Here are your pictures. They show **young people studying in different situations**.
	Indicate the pictures on page C1 to the candidates.
	I'd like you to compare two of the pictures, and say **how effective these ways of learning might be, and what difficulties the students might be experiencing.**
	All right?
Candidate A:	[*1 minute*]
Interlocutor:	Thank you.
	(Candidate B), **which learning experience do you think would be the most effective?** ...... **(Why?)**
Candidate B:	[*Approximately 30 seconds*]
Interlocutor:	Thank you.
	Now, *(Candidate B)*, here are your pictures. They show **friends spending time together.**
	Indicate the pictures on page C2 to the candidates.
	I'd like you to compare two of the pictures, and say **what you think the people might be talking about, and how important their friendship with each other might be.**
	All right?
Candidate B:	[*1 minute*]
Interlocutor:	Thank you.
	(Candidate A), **which friendship do you think might last the longest?** ...... **(Why?)**
Candidate A:	[*Approximately 30 seconds*]
Interlocutor:	Thank you.

Parts 3 and 4   8 minutes (12 minutes for groups of three)

The good life

Part 3

Interlocutor:	Now, I'd like you to talk about something together for about three minutes. *(5 minutes for groups of three)*
	Here are some pictures showing things that some people consider important for a good life.
	Indicate the pictures on C3 to the candidates.
	First, talk to each other about **why these things might be important for a good life.** Then decide **which one would bring the greatest long-term satisfaction.**
	All right?
Candidates:	[*3 minutes (5 minutes for groups of three)*]
Interlocutor:	Thank you.

Part 4

Interlocutor: *Select any of the following questions, as appropriate:*

- Do you think that we expect too much from life nowadays? ...... (Why? / Why not?)
- How do advertising and the media affect our expectations of a good life?
- The only thing people seem to be interested in nowadays is money. To what extent do you agree?
- How important is it to achieve a good balance between work and leisure in life?
- Some people say we have lost the ability to enjoy the simple things in life. What's your opinion?

> *Select any of the following prompts, as appropriate:*
> - What do you think?
> - Do you agree?
> - How about you?

Thank you. That is the end of the test.

Test 2

Note: In the examination, there will be both an assessor and an interlocutor in the room. The visual material for **Test 2** appears on pages C4 and C5 (Part 2), and C6 (Part 3).

Part 1   3 minutes (5 minutes for groups of three)

Interlocutor: Good morning/afternoon/evening. My name is .... and this is my colleague ....

And your names are?

Can I have your mark sheets, please?

Thank you.

First of all, we'd like to know something about you.

Select one or two questions and ask candidates in turn, as appropriate.

- Where are you from?
- What do you do here/there?
- How long have you been studying English?
- What do you enjoy most about learning English?

Select one or more questions from any of the following categories, as appropriate.

Entertainment and leisure

- Over the past few years, has the way you spend your leisure time changed very much?
- Would you say you spend too much time watching TV? ......
  (Why? / Why not?)

Making friends and meeting people

- How important is it to socialise with your friends? ...... (Why? /
  Why not?)
- What do you think is the best way to make friends? ...... (Why?)

Part 2   4 minutes (6 minutes for groups of three)

City life

Writing

Interlocutor:	In this part of the test, I'm going to give each of you three pictures. I'd like you to talk about them on your own for about a minute, and also to answer a question briefly about your partner's pictures.
	(Candidate A), it's your turn first. Here are your pictures. They show **people experiencing different aspects of city life.**
	Indicate the pictures on page C4 to the candidates.
	I'd like you to compare two of the pictures, and say **what aspects of city life the pictures show, and how the people might be feeling.**
	All right?
Candidate A:	[*1 minute*]
Interlocutor:	Thank you.
	(Candidate B), **which picture do you think best illustrates the disadvantages of city life?** ...... **(Why?)**
Candidate B:	[*Approximately 30 seconds*]
Interlocutor:	Thank you.
	Now, *(Candidate B)*, here are your pictures. They show **people writing in different situations.**
	Indicate the pictures on page C5 to the candidates.
	I'd like you to compare two of the pictures, and say **why the people might be writing in these situations, and how important it is for the people to write accurately.**
	All right?
Candidate B:	[*1 minute*]
Interlocutor:	Thank you.
	(Candidate A), **in which situation do you think it's most important to write accurately?** ...... **(Why?)**
Candidate A:	[*Approximately 30 seconds*]
Interlocutor:	Thank you.

Parts 3 and 4   8 minutes (12 minutes for groups of three)

Science museum

Part 3

Interlocutor:	Now, I'd like you to talk about something together for about three minutes. *(5 minutes for groups of three)*
	I'd like you to imagine that a museum wants to encourage young people to find out more about science. Here are some ideas they are considering.
	Indicate the pictures on page C6 to the candidates.
	First, talk to each other about how successful these activities might be in encouraging young people to find out more about science. Then decide which one would teach them the most.
	All right?
Candidates:	[*3 minutes (5 minutes for groups of three)*]
Interlocutor:	Thank you.

Part 4

Interlocutor: *Select any of the following questions, as appropriate:*

> *Select any of the following prompts, as appropriate:*
> - What do you think?
> - Do you agree?
> - How about you?

- What qualities do you think a person needs to become a successful scientist? ...... (Why?)
- Some people decide on their future career at a very early age. What are the advantages and disadvantages of this?
- How can teachers make a subject interesting for their students?
- How do you think technology will affect the way people learn in the future?
- What do you consider to be the most important scientific invention in the last fifty years? ...... (Why?)

Thank you. That is the end of the test.

Test 3

Note: In the examination, there will be both an assessor and an interlocutor in the room. The visual material for **Test 3** appears on pages C7 and C8 (Part 2), and C9 (Part 3).

Part 1   3 minutes (5 minutes for groups of three)

Interlocutor:	Good morning/afternoon/evening. My name is .... and this is my colleague ....

And your names are?

Can I have your mark sheets, please?

Thank you.

First of all, we'd like to know something about you.

Select one or two questions and ask candidates in turn, as appropriate.

- Where are you from?
- What do you do here/there?
- How long have you been studying English?
- What do you enjoy most about learning English?

Select one or more questions from any of the following categories, as appropriate.

Surroundings

- Which do you think is more important, the place you live in or the people you live with? ...... (Why?)
- What effect does the weather have on the way you feel?

Making friends and meeting people

- Are you the kind of person who enjoys meeting new people? ...... (Why? / Why not?)
- Is it better to have a few close friends or a wide circle of acquaintances? ...... (Why? / Why not?)

Part 2   4 minutes (6 minutes for groups of three)

Outdoor events

A sense of achievement

Interlocutor: In this part of the test, I'm going to give each of you three pictures. I'd like you to talk about them on your own for about a minute, and also to answer a question briefly about your partner's pictures.

(Candidate A), it's your turn first. Here are your pictures. They show **different outdoor events**.

Indicate the pictures on page C7 to the candidates.

I'd like you to compare two of the pictures, and say **why people organise events such as these, and what the atmosphere at the events might be like.**

All right?

Candidate A: [*1 minute*]

Interlocutor: Thank you.

(Candidate B), **which event do you think would be the most interesting to attend?** ...... (Why?)

Candidate B: [*Approximately 30 seconds*]

Interlocutor: Thank you.

Now, *(Candidate B)*, here are your pictures. They show **different situations in which people are trying to achieve something.**

Indicate the pictures on page C8 to the candidates.

I'd like you to compare two of the pictures, and say **what might motivate the people to do these things, and how difficult it might be for the people to achieve success.**

All right?

Candidate B: [*1 minute*]

Interlocutor: Thank you.

(Candidate A), **who do you think is most likely to achieve success?** ...... (Why?)

Candidate A: [*Approximately 30 seconds*]

Interlocutor: Thank you.

Parts 3 and 4   8 minutes (12 minutes for groups of three)

Childhood experiences

Part 3

Interlocutor:	Now, I'd like you to talk about something together for about three minutes. *(5 minutes for groups of three)*
	Here are some pictures showing different childhood experiences.
	Indicate the pictures on page C9 to the candidates.
	First, talk to each other about **what children might gain from these different experiences.** Then decide **which two might be the most useful for the children in their adult lives.**
	All right?
Candidates:	[*3 minutes (5 minutes for groups of three)*]
Interlocutor:	Thank you.

Part 4

Interlocutor: *Select any of the following questions, as appropriate:*

- Why do you think some people say that childhood is the best time of our lives?
- Some people say that young people have to study too hard these days. What's your opinion?
- Do you think people are born with creative skills or can these skills be learnt? ...... (Why? / Why not?)
- To what extent do you think young people are influenced by television? ...... (Why?)
- How are the lives of young people today different from those of their parents?

> *Select any of the following prompts, as appropriate:*
>
> - What do you think?
> - Do you agree?
> - How about you?

Thank you. That is the end of the test.

Test 4

Note: In the examination, there will be both an assessor and an interlocutor in the room. The visual material for **Test 4** appears on pages C10 and C11 (Part 2), and C12 (Part 3).

Part 1   3 minutes (5 minutes for groups of three)

Interlocutor:	Good morning/afternoon/evening. My name is .... and this is my colleague ....

And your names are?

Can I have your mark sheets, please?

Thank you.

First of all we'd like to know something about you.

Select one or two questions and ask candidates in turn, as appropriate.

- Where are you from?
- What do you do here/there?
- How long have you been studying English?
- What do you enjoy most about learning English?

Select one or more questions from any of the following categories, as appropriate.

Entertainment and leisure

- What would be your idea of a perfect day out? ...... (Why?)
- Do you prefer to watch a performance live or on TV? ...... (Why?)

Hopes and ambitions

- Do you think it's more important to be successful or to enjoy what you do? ...... (Why?)
- If you became rich and famous, do you think you would be happy? ...... (Why? / Why not?)

Part 2   4 minutes (6 minutes for groups of three)

Close to nature

After-school activities

Interlocutor:	In this part of the test, I'm going to give each of you three pictures. I'd like you to talk about them on your own for about a minute, and also to answer a question briefly about your partner's pictures.
	(Candidate A), it's your turn first. Here are your pictures. They show **people getting close to nature.**
	Indicate the pictures on page C10 to the candidates.
	I'd like you to compare two of the pictures, and say **what the people might be learning by getting close to nature in these ways, and how the people might be feeling.**
	All right?
Candidate A:	[*1 minute*]
Interlocutor:	Thank you.
	(Candidate B), **which experience do you think would be the most exciting? ...... (Why?)**
Candidate B:	[*Approximately 30 seconds*]
Interlocutor:	Thank you.
	Now, *(Candidate B)*, here are your pictures. They show **activities that students can choose to do after school.**
	Indicate the pictures on page C11 to the candidates.
	I'd like you to compare two of the pictures, and say **what students would learn from doing these activities after school, and how popular they might be with students.**
	All right?
Candidate B:	[*1 minute*]
Interlocutor:	Thank you.
	(Candidate A), **which activity do you think would be the most relaxing for students after studying all day? ...... (Why?)**
Candidate A:	[*Approximately 30 seconds*]
Interlocutor:	Thank you.

Parts 3 and 4   8 minutes (12 minutes for groups of three)

Modern technology

Part 3

Interlocutor:	Now, I'd like you to talk about something together for about three minutes. *(5 minutes for groups of three)*
	Here are some pictures showing different types of modern technology.
	Indicate the pictures on page C12 to the candidates.
	First, talk to each other about **what positive and negative effects these types of technology have had on people's lives.** Then decide **which type of technology might bring the greatest benefit to people in the future.**
	All right?
Candidates:	[*3 minutes (5 minutes for groups of three)*]
Interlocutor:	Thank you.

Part 4

Interlocutor: *Select any of the following questions, as appropriate:*

> *Select any of the following prompts, as appropriate:*
> - What do you think?
> - Do you agree?
> - How about you?

- Why do you think some people find it difficult to adapt to new technology?
- Some people say that technology like security cameras and computer databases are a threat to our freedom. What's your view?
- Do you think that technology will one day provide a solution to all the world's problems? ...... (Why? / Why not?)
- Some people say life was simpler in the past without modern technology. What's your opinion?
- Do you think that technology will result in more people being unemployed in the future? ...... (Why? / Why not?)

Thank you. That is the end of the test.

Marks and results

Paper 1 Reading

Candidates record their answers on a separate answer sheet. Two marks are given for each correct answer in **Parts 1, 2** and **3** and one mark is given for each correct answer in **Part 4**. The total score is then weighted to 40 marks for the whole Reading paper.

Paper 2 Writing

Examiners look at four aspects of a candidate's writing: Content, Language, Organisation and Communicative Achievement.

Content focuses on how well the candidate has fulfilled the task; in other words if they have done what they were asked to do.
Communicative Achievement focuses on how appropriate the writing is for the situation and whether the candidate has used the appropriate register.
Organisation focuses on the way the piece of writing was put together; in other words if it is logical and ordered, and the punctuation is correct.
Language focuses on the candidate's vocabulary and grammar. This includes the range of language as well as how accurate it is.

For each of the subscales, the examiner gives a maximum of 5 marks.

Examiners use the following assessment scale:

C1	Content	Communicative Achievement	Organisation	Language
5	All content is relevant to the task. Target reader is fully informed.	Uses the conventions of the communicative task with sufficient flexibility to communicate complex ideas in an effective way, holding the target reader's attention with ease, fulfilling all communicative purposes.	Text is a well-organised, coherent whole, using a variety of cohesive devices and organisational patterns with flexibility.	Uses a range of vocabulary, including less common lexis, effectively and precisely. Uses a wide range of simple and complex grammatical forms with full control, flexibility and sophistication. Errors, if present, are related to less common words and structures, or as slips.
4	*Performance shares features of Bands 3 and 5.*			
3	Minor irrelevances and/or omissions may be present. Target reader is, on the whole, informed.	Uses the conventions of the communicative task effectively to hold the target reader's attention and communicate straightforward and complex ideas, as appropriate.	Text is well organised and coherent, using a variety of cohesive devices and organisational patterns to generally good effect.	Uses a range of vocabulary, including less common lexis, appropriately. Uses a range of simple and complex grammatical forms with control and flexibility. Occasional errors may be present but do not impede communication.

2	*Performance shares features of Bands 1 and 3.*			
1	Irrelevances and misinterpretation of task may be present. Target reader is minimally informed.	Uses the conventions of the communicative task to hold the target reader's attention and communicate straightforward ideas.	Text is generally well organised and coherent, using a variety of linking words and cohesive devices.	Uses a range of everyday vocabulary appropriately, with occasional inappropriate use of less common lexis. Uses a range of simple and some complex grammatical forms with a good degree of control. Errors do not impede communication.
0	Content is totally irrelevant. Target reader is not informed.	*Performance below Band 1.*		

Length of responses

Candidates need to make sure that they write the correct number of words. Responses which are too short may not have an adequate range of language and may not provide all the information that is required. Responses which are too long may contain irrelevant content and have a negative effect on the reader.

Varieties of English

Candidates are expected to use a particular variety of English with some degree of consistency in areas such as spelling, and not for example switch from using a British spelling of a word to an American spelling of the same word.

Sample A (Test 1, Question 1 – Report)

This report aims to inform the Student Committee about my first week as a student at your college, where I was part of the Programm of Events for New Students.

MONDAY

First day of the College and exactly after the brekfast in the great hall, we did the college tour. Even thought the scenery and the buildings were great, I think I will have a big trouble remember it all. Owning a college map, would be really necessary.

TUESDAY

Today the meeting with tutors was organised. I have not only to admit that I received excellent information about each course, but I was also delighted to see such a helpful staff.

WEDNESDAY

Third day in the college, and we were asked whether we will participate in a club. I chose to join the basketball team. We were taken to the stadium. It is fantastic, but what is more is that I made some good friends.

THURSDAY

All the new students, including myself, were surprised to find out that a visit to the city-centre was organised! Despit the wonderful little shops and the big green parks, the tour on foot was exhausting. I think that a few brakes would be useful to the next year's students.

FRIDAY

In order to start with the best possible way our courses, the college had organised a party. The atmosphaire was great. The meals were great, and everyone had a very nice time. The only bad thing was that it finished too early …

To conclude, I thing that the activities orginised for the new student were overall wonderful. Thank you for accepting me and giving me the chance to have such a terrific time.

Scales	Mark	Commentary
Content	4	All content is relevant to the task. The target reader is fully informed about what was helpful on the course, and on the whole, informed about suggested changes for the future.
Communicative Achievement	2	The conventions of a report are used to hold the target reader's attention and communicate straightforward and complex ideas.
Organisation	3	The report is well organised and coherent, using cohesive devices and organisational patterns to generally good effect.
Language	2	Everyday vocabulary is used appropriately, and a range of simple and some complex grammatical forms is used. Errors are present but do not impede communication.

Sample B (Test 1, Question 4 – Article)

A Day As A Spiderman

If I was asked which film character I would like to be for a day then I would definitely go for Spiderman.

Besides being a symbol of justice and all that stuff what can be better than shooting web from your hands, have extreme acrobatic skills and make the city your own jungle. Not to mention testing your karate skills against criminals and fighting genetically manipulated foes. Personally, it fits my style and I have always been a fan of Spiderman.

I would like my day as Spiderman to be like this: I wake up at seven o'clock in the morning, have a quick breakfast and rush to work. There I am told that a giant snake looking criminal has appeared and is wreaking havok. So I assigned to go and get pictures. While on my way there, I get in a dark alley, I change clothes and become Spiderman.

The fight is tough and intense but in the end I am victorious. My automatic camera took great pictures which I later show to my directors. I am rewarded for my work and with the money I was given I take my girlfriend out at night. We go to a nice restaurant for dinner and then straight to the disco. The night was over before we knew it. I drive her home, kiss goodbye and go to my place to get some sleep.

That would be my perfect day as a Spiderman, full of action, adventure and romance.

Scales	Mark	Commentary
Content	5	All content is relevant to the task. The target reader is fully informed about why the writer would like to be this character for a day.
Communicative Achievement	5	The conventions of an article are used with sufficient flexibility to communicate complex ideas in an effective way, holding the target reader's attention with ease.
Organisation	4	The article is well organised and coherent, using a variety of cohesive devices and organisational patterns to good effect.
Language	4	A range of vocabulary (including less common lexis) is used effectively and precisely, and a range of complex grammatical forms is used with control and flexibility.

Sample C (Test 2, Question 1 – Proposal)

Film Club

Introduction

This proposal adresses the problem that the Saint Mary's college pays a lot of money in order to fund the Film Club although it has very few members.

Positive aspects

First of all, it has to be mentioned that every day in the Film Club quiz evenings are being held which have great appeal to the students of the college. Apart from that, over the last month we have welcomed 15 new members which means that the popularity of the club is being increased.

Recommendations

Firstly, as the entry fee is very small we could charge the students who come in order to enjoy their evenings in the Film Club a little more, so as to earn more money. Secondly, we could attract more people by organizing disco nights after 10pm. Also, as all the movies in the DVD library are old, it would be advisable to replace them or just add new ones which will definetely have an appeal to the college's students.

Conclusion

To conclude I strongly believe that the Saint Mary's college shouldn't reduce the funding to the Film Club because many of its students have a great time there and this is the only way for them to let off steam and escape for a while from the demanding subjects of the curriculum.

Scales	Mark	Commentary
Content	5	All content is relevant to the task. The target reader is fully informed.
Communicative Achievement	3	The conventions of a proposal are used effectively to hold the target reader's attention and communicate complex ideas.
Organisation	4	The proposal is well organised and coherent, using a variety of cohesive devices and organisational patterns to good effect.
Language	4	A range of vocabulary is used effectively, and a range of grammatical forms is used with control and flexibility.

Sample D (Test 2, Question 4 – Review)

During the last decade magazines which have as main topic computers and technology have been increasing in number. Only "PC World" however is the number-one in quality pc magazine since its first release seven years ago.

"PC World" is one of the most popular magazines ready by young people. Since I've never missed an issue I'm the appropriate to explain why. Every month, you can read the articles for new pc components and be well-informed by the analytical tests and benchmarks performed by the editors and special staff. Apart from pc articles there are standard parts of every issue which present new technologies, video games, smartphones and also provide other interesting technology related reviews and previews.

You may say that the above can be found in other magazines. Well, "PC World" is not only the 130 page issue you buy every month. It gives you a CD-ROM with many fully functional programmes and games to keep you in front of your computer by the arrival of the next edition. Moreover by visiting the PC-World website, you find up-to-date information and articles for new products and download updated software.

Nevertheless, as nothing is perfect, our favourite magazine has its flaws. It would be a great feature if it could provide some articles not so oriented to technology freaks. Many of my friends find it difficult to understand the terminology used in most texts. Also, it is important to be released in electronic version so that it is available to members online. Finally a price drop would be welcome especially for students who cannot afford it every month.

Despite these little disadvantages, all of us who support "PC World" since its birth, will continue doing so. For everyone who wants to enter our "World" we will offer our support through the website forum.

Scales	Mark	Commentary
Content	5	All content is relevant to the task. The target reader is fully informed about why the magazine is popular and how it could be improved.
Communicative Achievement	5	The conventions of a review are used with sufficient flexibility to communicate complex ideas in an effective way, holding the target reader's attention with ease.
Organisation	4	The review is well organised and coherent, using a variety of cohesive devices and organisational patterns to good effect.
Language	4	A range of vocabulary (including less common lexis) is used effectively and precisely, and a range of simple and complex grammatical forms is used with control and flexibility.

Sample E (Test 3, Question 2 – Article)

> *Too little too late?*
>
> *People who are outside of my country would be amazed how we follow detailed instructions for each item of rubbish to be recycled – bottles in one bin, paper in another. However, we do this because we want our rubbish to be collected, not due to any concern about global warming.*
>
> *Personally, I think the majority of people couldn't care less about the Earth – we often hear on the news announcements about global warming, and although some make efforts like keeping their air conditioner level low in summer in offices and at home, we still see bright lights everywhere and consume a high amount of natural resources.*
>
> *I do care about global warming too, and I do what I can, but do these small efforts make any diffrence? I feel worried when I watch science or nature programs and learn what is actually happening to our planet. I understand that the Earth is in a great danger but nevertheless our life seems to go on comfortably. This is the main reason why people hasn't reacted the way we should. People still drive cars with big engines and fly on holiday to other countries – don't we have to stop these as well as recycling responsibly and buying 'greener' products? I think the problem is that although we hear a lot about global warming, we don't really see its effects so we don't take it seriously. Let's hope we're not too late.*

Scales	Mark	Commentary
Content	5	All content is relevant to the task. The target reader is fully informed.
Communicative Achievement	3	The conventions of an article are used effectively to hold the target reader's attention and communicate straightforward and complex ideas.
Organisation	3	The article is well organised and coherent, using a variety of cohesive devices and organisational patterns to generally good effect.
Language	2	A range of vocabulary, including less common lexis, is used appropriately, and a range of simple and some grammatical forms is used with a good degree of control. Errors do not impede communication.

Sample F (Test 3, Question 3 – Essay)

> Over the last 50 years more and more communication is done by computer. This includes email, skype and social networking like Facebook.
>
> I feel that there are lots of advantages in communicating with each other by computer. Firstly, it takes hardly any time at all to get in touch with your friends and family, which is convenient as we are all spending more time away from each other and overseas. Furthermore, the 'global village' means we know people from many countries, and only technology lets us manage friends all round the world. In our parents' time they had to write paper letters which used to take days or weeks to arrive, but they might say real letters are more personal.
>
> Besides, computers are also used to make phone calls. This is often completely free – you just need a fast internet connection and you can make a video call and see the face of the person you're talking to, which seemed like a dream only twenty years ago. But this does not replace phones – computers are too big to be carried and used all the time, which means handies especially smartphones will always be popular, despite they are very expensive.
>
> The most amazing development has been social networking, such as Facebook. Using this we can communicate with many people at the same time rather than just one-to-one. I think this factor is the biggest advantage for using computers and I wonder what will come next. However, it would be good if computers got cheaper so everyone can afford to enjoy them.

Scales	Mark	Commentary
Content	5	All content is relevant to the task. The target reader is fully informed.
Communicative Achievement	3	The conventions of an essay are used effectively to hold the target reader's attention and communicate straightforward and complex ideas.
Organisation	2	The essay is well organised and coherent, using a variety of linking words and cohesive devices.
Language	3	A range of vocabulary, including less common lexis, is used appropriately. A range of simple and complex grammatical forms is used with control and flexibility. Occasional errors do not impede communication.

Sample G (Test 4, Question 1 – Proposal)

Dear Masters,

In responce to your email I am writing to inform you of the best event for the End of the Year Celebration. Bearing in mind that the students are not wealthy but want something special for the Celebration I will try to propose the event that fits best to their expectations.

Disco and barbecue party in college

First of all, creating a disco inside the college would be a great idea. In my opinion dancing is loved by every student and it is an easy way to relax and have fun. The disco could be supported by a barbecue and as you know most of the students love this kind of food.

Coach trip to Dublin

Secondly, another excellent idea is to organize an excursion to Dublin. The trip is better than the previous idea because shy students would not be able to dance at all. By the time the students arrive there they are free to go for shopping or for sightseeing or do any activity that gives them pleasure.

A visit to the theatre and meal in a restaurant

Finally, I would be glad to propose a visit to our local theatre. There are some wonderful plays to watch and some of them can teach a lot to students about society, life and the environment. Moreover, after leaving from there the children can be brought to a fine restaurant with good prices so that they can eat and rest after a tiring day.

Conclusion

I hope that my recommendation about the theatre and the restaurant will prove to be an unforgettable experience for all the students.

Yours faithfully

Scales	Mark	Commentary
Content	1	"Explaining why you think it would be the most suitable event" is only minimally addressed, and "suggesting how it could be organised" is omitted. Target reader is minimally informed.
Communicative Achievement	2	Uses the conventions of the report to hold the target reader's attention and communicate straightforward and some more complex ideas.
Organisation	2	Text is well organised and coherent, using a variety of linking words and cohesive devices to generally good effect.
Language	2	Uses a range of everyday vocabulary appropriately. Uses a range of simple and some complex grammatical forms with a good degree of control.

Sample H (Test 4, Question 4 – Contribution)

> *Dear Editor,*
>
> *I am writing in response to the article, which was announced on the newspaper "Times" on the 4th of November, was about a research into different transport problems and I would like to contribute to this research.*
>
> *First of all, I would like to say that our country faces many transport problems. The biggest problem is with the bus transport. Due to the hustle and bustle of the big cities the buses delay in the streets and most of the people that have to attend meetings strugle to be on time. The same happens and with the taxes or even with the cars and most of people are completely discouraged with this situation.*
>
> *Many facts have caused this problem. One of them is that nowadays the percentage of cars in the streets has risen and traffic can not be avoid. So, people that have no other choice than to use bus transportation strugle to be on time for their work.*
>
> *In order to solve this problem the mayor should take action. One way to reduce traffic would be to encourage people to use more the buses, so as the car traffic to be redused and so as buses to be able to transport people without hours of delay.*
>
> *To summarise, not only in our country but all over the world there is a serious problem of transportation and the mayors or even better the government should take action. I hope you take my letter into serious consideration.*
>
> *Yours faithfully*

Scales	Mark	Commentary
Content	4	All content is relevant to the task. Target reader is informed. There is some over-reliance on the point about struggling to be on time.
Communicative Achievement	2	Uses the conventions of a letter to hold the target reader's attention and communicate straightforward and some more complex ideas.
Organisation	1	Text is well organised and coherent, using a variety of linking words and cohesive devices.
Language	1	Uses a range of everyday vocabulary appropriately, with occasional inappropriate use of less common lexis. Uses a range of simple and some complex grammatical forms with a good degree of control. Errors do not impede communication.

Paper 3   Use of English

One mark is given for each correct answer in **Parts 1, 2** and **3**. Two marks are given for each correct answer in **Part 4**. For **Part 5**, candidates are awarded a mark of 2, 1 or 0 for each question according to the accuracy of their response. Correct spelling is required in **Parts 2, 3, 4** and **5**. The total mark is subsequently weighted to 40.

Paper 4   Listening

One mark is given for each correct answer. The total is weighted to give a mark out of 40 for the paper.

For security reasons, several versions of the Listening paper are used at each administration of the examination. Before grading, the performance of the candidates in each of the versions is compared and marks adjusted to compensate for any imbalance in levels of difficulty.

Paper 5   Speaking

Candidates are assessed on their own individual performance and not in relation to each other, according to the following five analytical criteria: grammatical resource, vocabulary resource, discourse management, pronunciation and interactive communication. Assessment is based on performance in the whole test and not in particular parts of the test.

Both examiners assess the candidates. The assessor applies detailed analytical scales, and the interlocutor applies a global achievement scale, which is based on the analytical scales.

Analytical scales

Grammatical resource

This refers to the accurate and appropriate use of a range of both simple and complex forms. Performance is viewed in terms of the overall effectiveness of the language used in spoken interaction.

Vocabulary resource

This refers to the candidate's ability to use a wide range of vocabulary to meet task requirements. At CAE level, the tasks require candidates to speculate and exchange views on unfamiliar topics. Performance is viewed in terms of the overall effectiveness of the language used in spoken interaction.

Discourse management

This refers to the candidate's ability to link utterances together to form coherent speech, without undue hesitation. The utterances should be relevant to the tasks and should be arranged logically to develop the themes or arguments required by the tasks.

Pronunciation

This refers to the candidate's ability to produce intelligible utterances to fulfil the task requirements. This includes stress and intonation as well as individual sounds. Examiners put themselves in the position of the non-ESOL specialist and assess the overall impact of the pronunciation and the degree of effort required to understand the candidate.

Interactive communication

This refers to the candidate's ability to take an active part in the development of the discourse. This requires the ability to participate in the range of interactive situations in the test and to develop discussions on a range of topics by initiating and responding appropriately. This also refers to the deployment of strategies to maintain interaction at an appropriate level throughout the test so that the tasks can be fulfilled.

Global achievement

This refers to the candidate's overall effectiveness in dealing with the tasks in the four separate parts of the CAE Speaking test. The global mark is an independent, impression mark which reflects the assessment of the candidate's performance from the interlocutor's perspective.

Marks

Marks for each of the criteria are awarded out of a five-point scale. Marks for the Speaking test are subsequently weighted to produce a final mark out of 40.

CAE typical minimum adequate performance

The candidate develops the interaction with contributions which are mostly coherent and extended when dealing with the CAE-level tasks. Grammar is mostly accurate and vocabulary appropriate. Utterances are understood with very little strain on the listener.

Test 1 Key

Paper 1   Reading (1 hour 15 minutes)

Part 1

1 D   2 C   3 D   4 A   5 B   6 C

Part 2

7 E   8 F   9 A   10 B   11 D   12 G

Part 3

13 B   14 B   15 C   16 B   17 D   18 A   19 A

Part 4

20 B   21 D   22 C   23 E   24 B   25 C   26 E   27 A   28 D   29 C
30 C   31 D   32 E   33 A   34 D

Paper 2   Writing (1 hour 30 minutes)

Candidate responses are marked using the assessment scale on pages 122–123.

Paper 3   Use of English (1 hour)

Part 1

1 C   2 A   3 D   4 C   5 D   6 B   7 D   8 C   9 B   10 A   11 C   12 B

Part 2

13 the   14 be   15 as   16 them   17 of   18 since   19 from   20 whose
21 up   22 Although / Though / While / Whilst   23 a   24 which   25 on
26 where   27 Even

Part 3

28 basis   29 cascading   30 comparison   31 considerable   32 numerous
33 depth   34 additional   35 enables   36 relatively   37 increasingly

Part 4

38 heavy   39 film   40 working   41 raised   42 drew

Part 5

43 her flu / the flu / having flu I Lucy MANAGED to pass   44 agreement had been/was
REACHED I about / on   45 order to AVOID I leaving OR an attempt / an effort to AVOID
I leaving   46 FAR too expensive I for Colin to   47 brother's ACCOUNT I of   48 little
LIKELIHOOD I of (our/us) seeing OR (that) we will see / we'll see   49 have been IMPOSED
I as a   50 for I your HELP / the HELP you gave me

Paper 4   Listening (approximately 40 minutes)

Part 1

1 A   2 C   3 B   4 C   5 A   6 C

Part 2

7 accountant   8 pressure   9 12 / twelve (huge) trees   10 (his) (own) electricity
11 (warm) (golden) brown   12 rope(s)   13 (enough) exercise   14 (personal) journey

Part 3

15 B   16 D   17 D   18 C   19 A   20 B

Part 4

21 D   22 H   23 G   24 B   25 C   26 B   27 A   28 H   29 D   30 F

Transcript	*This is the Cambridge Certificate in Advanced English Listening Test. Test One.*
	I am going to give you the instructions for this test. I shall introduce each part of the test and give you time to look at the questions.
	At the start of each piece, you will hear this sound:
	tone
	You will hear each piece twice.
	Remember, while you are listening, write your answers on the question paper. You will have five minutes at the end of the test to copy your answers onto the separate answer sheet.
	There will now be a pause. Please ask any questions now, because you must not speak during the test.
	[pause]
PART 1	*Now open your question paper and look at Part One.*
	[pause]
	You will hear three different extracts. For questions 1 to 6, choose the answer (A, B, or C) which fits best according to what you hear. There are two questions for each extract.
Extract 1	*You overhear two friends talking about holidays.*
	Now look at questions one and two.
	[pause]
	tone

Woman:	Hi, how are you? Still saving the planet?
Man:	Hello! Thinking about holidays actually. Though I'm very glad to say that since I last saw you I've been cycling to work, sorting the rubbish – I've even got a compost heap! It all takes time and a lot of energy – especially the bike! I'm ready for a change, something different. I suppose I should go off on some work camp in the country – you know, cleaning out canals, mending hedges, that sort of thing? What do you think?
Woman:	No, no – far too extreme. Remember the big polluter is air travel – so be an eco-traveller – you can easily go all around Europe without boarding a plane at all. Don't forget trains, ferries, coaches. And when you are abroad, spread the tourism pound around. Don't stay in multi-national hotels – choose locally run guest houses and hotels and eat in local restaurants. Buy food and souvenirs from markets or craft co-operatives rather than hotel lobby shops. That way you'll be continuing the good work – and you'll get a decent vacation.

[pause]

tone

[The recording is repeated.]

[pause]

Extract 2   *You hear part of an interview with a woman called Jane Hilton, who takes part in the sport of free climbing. Now look at questions three and four.*

[pause]

tone

Interviewer:	Jane, tell us what you do.
Woman:	It's called free climbing – I just use finger strength and balance, not climbing equipment. Of course, there's a rope to catch me if I slip – which in free climbing happens frequently – but otherwise, it's just me and the rock. It's more like chess than a dangerous sport – there's so much strategy and skill involved. One of my first climbs was a huge rock that some people considered impossible to get up because of its steep flat surfaces. It took ages, but once I'd done it I felt I just had to climb it again – just for fun.
Interviewer:	What drives you?
Woman:	When I was young I had this reputation for rebelling against tradition. It wasn't exactly true, but I just thought, 'well if I'm different then I'll just be me and do what I feel like doing'. I think making that choice gave me a certain freedom to do what I liked, and this was a bonus that I could do an activity that meant something to me. When I finally reach the point where I can see the landscape spread out below me, it brings tears to my eyes. I hope that it's something I'll keep doing for years!

[pause]

tone

[The recording is repeated.]

[pause]

Extract 3
       You overhear part of a conversation about diving in underwater forests of kelp, which is a type of marine plant.

       Now look at questions five and six.

       [pause]

       tone

Man:	You know, coming to California eight years ago was just a revelation for me, after the coral reefs of Florida.
Woman:	Yeah?
Man:	I didn't know there were these giant kelp forests underwater here. Now I like kelp diving best of all. I usually dive to the bottom of the seabed and look up at the sunlight coming down through the plants.
Woman:	It's awesome. You don't just swim past the scenery, you're in it. You're like birds flying through the forest. Well, OK, you have a little more than feathers to keep you moving!
Man:	And penetrating a kelp forest is actually not that hard once you know how, wouldn't you say?
Woman:	There's pretty much always a way through. The hitch is that you and your buddy …
Man:	Your diving partner, yeah.
Woman:	… have to go in single file.
Man:	Which makes it easy for you to get separated, and you have to watch your air supply. There's no way you can share it!
Woman:	And if you make the mistake of using your fins too hard, that sucks the kelp towards you. Still, you learn not to, pretty fast!
Man:	What I found last week was …

       [pause]

       tone

       [The recording is repeated.]

       [pause]

       That is the end of Part One.
       Now turn to Part Two.

       [pause]

PART 2
       You will hear a man called Kevin Riley talking about his unusual home in Australia. For questions 7 to 14, complete the sentences.

       You now have 45 seconds to look at Part Two.

       [pause]

       tone

Kevin:	If you met me in the street today, I think you'd find me a relaxed kind of guy, at ease with myself – you might not even believe I run a chain of macrobiotic restaurants. But fifteen years ago … well, I was a highly stressed accountant in Australia – a real high flyer – and over the years, I began to hate the routine of my job … crazy deadlines to meet. I even got tired of the life style: expense account lunches, a smart apartment.

It all changed one day when I got talking to a friend of mine, an architect who studies the homes of indigenous peoples, and found some interesting ideas about the relationship between people and their environment. They believe a building should put as little pressure on the earth as possible – that's why in my house, only stilt-like supports make contact with the ground.

Anyway, this friend really inspired me … so, I bought some woodland on a hill above Sydney and cleared most of the site myself. But it took fifteen men to cut down the twelve huge trees on the site, and it was important for me that *they* felt what they were doing was meaningful too. I wanted the place to be filled with positive energy right from the beginning, so, I used the trunks of those trees to build the supports for the house.

It's still quite an adventure to get to my house. First there's a very steep driveway. You get out of the car by a small hut where I generate my own electricity. Stacked outside, you'll find the surfboards I make use of in my free time! This is Australia after all. Then there are rocks and walkways across the stream to reach the house.

It's small and simple ... but it's just right, on three floors. It's made mainly of wood – originally light-brown coloured ash and pink-coloured gum wood – but with time, both have gradually mellowed to the same warm golden brown. It's so easy to maintain inside – I just wash the whole place down from time to time with a hose!

Let me describe the top floor to give you some idea of what it's like. Three of the walls consist of large, sliding glass windows, which can be pushed back so you're right in the tree-tops. The fourth wall is made up of sliding wooden panels that conceal a small cabin bedroom and bathroom. The main room is very simply furnished with a low wooden bed, a hammock and a chair made of driftwood and rope. Nothing extra.

Most people spend their lives half asleep – I know I used to – weighed down with rich food and never getting enough exercise, but now I get something positive out of every day. I'm not waiting months to have a holiday and a change of scene because I love where I live. I'm in touch with the elements and everything that is going on around me. Building the house was a bit like a personal journey and now I've arrived at a place where I feel calm and comfortable.

[pause]

Now you will hear Part Two again.

tone

[The recording is repeated.]

[pause]

That is the end of Part Two.
Now turn to Part Three.

[pause]

PART 3   *You will hear an interview with a man called Seth Jeavons, who organises an annual three-day pop-music festival. For questions 15 to 20, choose the answer (A, B, C or D) which fits best according to what you hear.*

You now have one minute to look at Part Three.

[pause]

tone

Interviewer: My guest today is Seth Jeavons, organiser of a large three-day pop-music festival. Seth, what should people bear in mind, especially those who are going to camp at the festival site? Have you got any tips?

Seth: Yes. The first thing is, although it's held in June, you can never rely on the local weather. Basics are – check that your tent is intact before you go – it'll keep you sheltered from wind, rain and a drop in temperature at night, but unfortunately what's often overlooked is that the terrain is really uneven at the site so you definitely need some sort of mattress. Even the smallest of tents can be adequate if it's good quality. Most areas are lit so bringing a torch, although not a bad idea, isn't essential.

Interviewer: There were a few criticisms of last year's festival, weren't there? Have you managed to put those right?

Seth: Some of the complaints were well-founded and we've worked hard to put those problems right. There again, some people said they were straining to hear the bands while others said they were being deafened, and that's just different expectations of noise levels. Where you stand when there's a huge audience can affect how well you hear too; that's why you get a bunching up of people standing in the middle. One concern we did have to address though was that of fans mobbing their favourite bands on stage. We've improved the cordon around the stage for the protection of both the fans and the bands. But I'm afraid the car park issue remains unresolved; we can't compromise on the space for camping and the space for people to watch the bands in reasonable comfort.

Interviewer: And do you think it's a good idea to bring children to the festival or not?

Seth: Absolutely. Naturally, we've got all the usual treats for them: a circus, a magic show, children's theatre and so on, and lots of food outlets offer kids' menus. What puts us above the rest though is that we've got crèches where parents can happily leave their children while they go off for an hour or so, because all our childminders are accredited by the National Childminding Agency. We also recommend that families, if they're camping, use the part of the field away from the main stage.

Interviewer: And who do you think is going to steal the show this year?

Seth: Well, the seemingly obvious answer would be the big-name bands. The thing is, they can be seen in most places most of the time, so I'd say the artists whose appearances on stage are rather infrequent will be the ones that people flock to. The audiences here are very discerning; they won't be fooled by the glitter and razzmatazz that some bands rely on. They want to hear good musicians play good music rather than have a poor band try to win them over with sing-alongs and lots of 'cosy' chats with the audience.

Interviewer:	These days, of course, with the Internet, you could argue that you don't really need to go to the festival, you can watch it, read blogs about it, etc.
Seth:	The TV coverage this year will be comprehensive with some gigs broadcast live and others recorded so that they can be shown later. But curled up on your sofa, you won't be part of it; you won't be able to look back in ten years' time and instantly relive the moment. True, people can download what they like on the Internet: amateur film, blogs and so on – even shots of some of the more unusual people in the audience, but I'm not sure of the legal position on that.
Interviewer:	So, the festival lives on. Are you thinking of making any changes for next year?
Seth:	My daughter Sarah is managing a whole section herself this year and it's been rumoured that I'm planning to hand over full responsibility to her eventually, but let's not go into that now. We'll keep to the same number of events, stages and fields as this year; I can't remember how many that is off the top of my head. Even the main band has already been booked – and the name's been leaked to the press. Some people complain about the annual hike in ticket prices but I'm afraid that's out of our hands. We have to pay whatever the going rate is for bands – and they never get cheaper.

[pause]

Now you will hear Part Three again.

tone

[The recording is repeated.]

[pause]

That is the end of Part Three.
Now turn to Part Four.

[pause]

PART 4

Part Four consists of two tasks. You will hear five short extracts in which people are talking about photography courses they have taken. Look at Task One. For questions 21 to 25, choose from the list (A to H) each speaker's occupation. Now look at Task Two. For questions 26 to 30, choose from the list (A to H) what each speaker appreciated most about their photography course. While you listen, you must complete both tasks.

You now have 45 seconds to look at Part Four.

[pause]

tone

| Speaker One: | I remember how dubious I was about choosing a course on the web. I mean, choosing anything on the web is risky. But to my delight, we all got a first-class course at an affordable rate. My career has taken me a bit away from photography, but not completely. Whenever I travel, I take snaps of everything: statues, unusual structures, gardens. And it's surprising how often I use them for inspiration, like with the design of a school with a totally new approach to education that we worked on recently. We had to work hard to marry innovative construction with the practicalities of accommodating fifteen hundred children. |

[pause]

Speaker Two: The thing I'll always remember from my course is how much difference Sean's comments on my work made. He used to speak to each of his students personally and would tell us exactly where we were going wrong. Take me, for example, I cover long distances and the regulations say I have to take regular breaks, which I use as photo opportunities. Before the course, I'd snapped away but with no sense of composition and was always a bit disappointed with the results. Now, I'm so enthusiastic that I'm encouraging my own kids to try photography. And you know what? They're producing highly original stuff; it's great! Even when I'm back behind the wheel on Mondays, it brings a smile to my face.

[pause]

Speaker Three: People didn't believe me when I said I was doing a photography course to help me with my job. They couldn't see the connection between dealing with copyright cases and photography – not until I pointed out that I often have to take photos of products when one company is accusing another of making fakes – a bit like being an undercover reporter. Doing the coursework was stimulating. I think of myself as quite intelligent but I can tell you some of the coursework we had to do really left me scratching my head! And when I looked back at the quality of the photos I took, I realised what an amazing course I'd found.

[pause]

Speaker Four: Everyone on the course, tutors and students, was tremendously busy and one hundred per cent involved. But I wasn't that impressed with the time it took for my tutor to get replies to my questions back to me. I mean, the course was fantastically interesting, it also made me look again at the way I worked in the classroom, and made me question whether I met the same professional standards myself. I was amazed that so many topics could be covered, and students were left with a feeling of having a good basis that they could always build on and develop their own unique style.

[pause]

Speaker Five: Funnily enough, doing the course has led to some developments in my own work. I'm working on a huge clay turtle at the moment, which I'm hoping will be chosen for a big exhibition in the summer. And now that I can take really professional looking photos of my work, it's so much easier to get positive replies from exhibition organisers and galleries. A couple of the others on the course had much more experience than me and they provided me with a wealth of tips about how to make a photo say what you want it to say. In fact, they were so good I sometimes wondered why they were doing the course.

[pause]

tone

Now you will hear Part Four again.

[The recording is repeated.]

[pause]

That is the end of Part Four.

There'll now be a pause of five minutes for you to copy your answers onto the separate answer sheet. Be sure to follow the numbering of all the questions. I shall remind you when there is one minute left, so that you are sure to finish in time.

[Teacher, pause the recording here for five minutes. Remind your students when they have one minute left.]

That is the end of the test. Please stop now. Your supervisor will now collect all the question papers and answer sheets.

Test 2 Key

Paper 1   Reading (1 hour 15 minutes)

Part 1

1 C   2 C   3 D   4 B   5 A   6 B

Part 2

7 G   8 D   9 B   10 E   11 A   12 F

Part 3

13 D   14 A   15 D   16 D   17 A   18 C   19 C

Part 4

20 B   21 D   22 A   23 C   24 D   25 B   26 A   27 B   28 D   29 A
30 C   31 B   32 A   33 B   34 A

Paper 2   Writing (1 hour 30 minutes)

Candidate responses are marked using the assessment scale on pages 122–123.

Paper 3   Use of English (1 hour)

Part 1

1 B   2 A   3 C   4 D   5 B   6 A   7 B   8 D   9 C   10 D
11 C   12 B

Part 2

13 while / whilst / when / if   14 Now / Today / Nowadays   15 why   16 but /
although / though   17 to   18 There   19 not / less   20 unless   21 of /
about   22 are   23 and   24 too   25 another   26 which   27 can / will

Part 3

28 availability   29 popularised / popularized   30 handle   31 reluctance   32 terrified
33 thankfully   34 ensure   35 stability   36 expertise   37 addictive

Part 4

38 matches   39 grown   40 form   41 put   42 tight

Part 5

43 isn't/won't be | the FIRST time / occasion   44 CAN be repaired / fixed (by him) | or
45 couldn't / didn't MANAGE | to get   46 will be / get BEATEN | by Portugal in   47 few
(boys / of them) | have (ever) HEARD of / about   48 MUST have forgotten | about / (that) he
was   49 no INTENTION (at all) | of returning / going back   50 under the IMPRESSION |
(that) it would

Paper 4   Listening (approximately 40 minutes)

Part 1

1 C   2 A   3 A   4 B   5 B   6 A

Part 2

7 bone(s)   8 inexpensive / cheap / not expensive   9 mouth piece / mouthpiece
10 market / market place / marketplace   11 Ireland   12 (new) rail / railway / train / railroad
station   13 compulsory / obligatory / mandatory / necessary   14 punctuation (marks)

Part 3

15 B   16 C   17 D   18 C   19 A   20 D

Part 4

21 C   22 B   23 H   24 A   25 F   26 F   27 D   28 G   29 B   30 H

Transcript	*This is the Cambridge Certificate in Advanced English Listening Test. Test Two.*
	I am going to give you the instructions for this test. I shall introduce each part of the test and give you time to look at the questions.
	At the start of each piece you will hear this sound:
	tone
	You will hear each piece twice.
	*Remember, while you are listening, write your answers on the **question paper**. You will have five minutes at the end of the test to copy your answers onto the separate answer sheet.*
	There will now be a pause. Please ask any questions now, because you must not speak during the test.
	[pause]
PART 1	*Now open your question paper and look at Part One.*
	[pause]
	You will hear three different extracts. For questions 1 to 6, choose the answer (A, B, or C) which fits best according to what you hear. There are two questions for each extract.
Extract 1	*You overhear a football fan talking to a friend about a new stadium he's just been to.*
	Now look at questions one and two.
	[pause]
	tone
Woman:	So, what did you think of the new stadium?
Man:	You should go; I mean it's the stadium of sporting dreams. The design is obviously very high-tech; it's really impressive though surprisingly subdued

when it comes to colour. The architect's deliberately worked with neutral tones because he reckons that the events themselves will provide enough life and excitement. At night, a central tower lights up like a beacon so everyone can see not just where it is but also how important it is, both to the local community and to the sport of football itself.

Woman: And what's it like inside?

Man: It's like a kind of swooping, smooth concrete arena wrapped around with five levels of atriums, walkways, cafés, shops. It's got the feel of an airport, not so much because of all those lofty interiors, but because absolutely no expense has been spared in the choice of seating, washrooms and refreshment areas. And they've got to be good because they'll have to stand up to the wear and tear that 90,000 people will impose.

[pause]

tone

[The recording is repeated.]

[pause]

Extract 2   *You hear part of an interview with the presenter of a breakfast radio programme.*

Now look at questions three and four.

[pause]

tone

Interviewer: What amazes me about your radio programme is that after all these years, you sound so cheerful and up for it at 6.30 in the morning! Surely there must be mornings when you think: 'I don't want to do this.'

Sarah: Well, I'm a performer, aren't I? I get a buzz out of it. I mean, on dark winter mornings it can be a bit hard, but I still come in with a spring in my step. So provided I'm healthy enough to do it, I'll carry on. But I know they'll eventually find someone younger to do the job – I have no illusions about that. One of my colleagues maybe …

Interviewer: Well, if your colleague John took over, that would be a huge change. You don't swear like he does, for one thing – I rather thought you disapproved of that.

Sarah: Well, he's an incredible risk taker … he's brave enough to open his mouth without knowing what he's going to say. Yet funnily enough people rarely take offence at what comes out. You'd think they would, but in fact they like him all the more for it. I've heard him do stuff that I certainly wouldn't attempt.

[pause]

tone

[The recording is repeated.]

[pause]

Extract 3   *You overhear two friends called Greg and Tamsin discussing a newspaper article about something called a seed bank.*

Now look at questions five and six.

[pause]

tone

Tamsin:	Have you read this article, Greg? About the three million seed varieties they've stored in a vault near the North Pole?
Greg:	I only glanced at it really. What's the seed bank for then?
Tamsin:	To, you know, back up the whole genetic diversity thing. The article says that farmers these days prefer modern higher-yield, disease-resistant species, so the more traditional varieties might disappear completely one day.
Greg:	I see. Sounds like a pretty valuable resource. It'll probably have loads of cameras and barbed wire and stuff to protect it.
Tamsin:	Nothing about that here – it says the people in charge are just going to find someone to keep an eye on the place, pass by once a week or so.
Greg:	Hmm, I reckon they'll get caught out there. Not that it'll be hard to find a suitable caretaker if that's all you have to do! So, have they decided actually how and when they'll supply the seeds?
Tamsin:	There's a whole paragraph on that. Here, you can read it.
Greg:	Right, thanks.

[pause]

tone

[The recording is repeated.]

[pause]

That is the end of Part One.
Now turn to Part Two.

[pause]

PART 2   *You will hear a musician called Barbara Devlin talking about the instrument she plays, which is called the penny whistle. For questions 7 to 14, complete the sentences.*

You now have 45 seconds to look at Part Two.

[pause]

tone

Musician:	I'm Barbara Devlin and I'm here to play an instrument called the penny whistle for you. But before I do that, let me tell you something about its history. In its present form, the instrument goes back to the mid 19th century; to the English village of Colney Weston. There in 1843, a farm labourer called Robert Dark invented what is actually a very simple type of flute. The basic idea was nothing new in the 19th century, though, and Robert had already got a wooden whistle of a type that had been in use for hundreds of years. Indeed, similar instruments carved out of bone have been discovered during archaeological excavations – some dating back to the 12th century.

But what Robert Dark invented was an instrument made out of metal. He had got hold of some tin, which was a relatively plentiful metal at that time, and therefore inexpensive. He experimented to see whether it would be possible to make a whistle out of it. To his surprise, it worked very well; the only non-metal part of the instrument being the mouthpiece – which Robert carved out of wood.

As well as finding the material, Robert also helped to make the instrument popular. After a disagreement with his employer, he decided to walk to the fast-growing industrial city of Manchester in search of a new life. There were few shops in those days, and most people lived in the countryside, so whenever he came to a village with a market place, Robert would stop and sell his whistles to the farm workers who gathered there. The whistles were popular, not least because they only cost a penny each – and the name 'penny whistle' stuck.

Many of these agricultural workers were from Ireland, doing seasonal work in England. There had always been a great enthusiasm there for whistle playing, much more so than in Scotland or Wales for example, and so when they went home, they took a penny whistle with them.

Once Robert arrived in Manchester – a good place to be, at the centre of a growing road and canal network – he cleverly predicted future developments and rented a little building just round the corner from the new railway station. This became his factory and he began making penny whistles in large quantities. And so it was that the penny whistle was introduced to the world.

So, what's it like to play? The whistle requires players to breathe correctly – it's the first thing you have to learn if you want to play one. If you can read sheet music, then tunes for the whistle are marked with breath marks – but these are not compulsory – because each person needs to find their own best breathing pattern – but they are useful. I always think that the breath mark is rather like the punctuation in a piece of written language; it tells you where it would be a good place to pause, in order to get the best sense out of the words. It's the same with music. So, if you're all ready, I'll give you a little tune to show you what I mean. This one's called …

[pause]

Now you will hear Part Two again.

tone

[The recording is repeated.]

[pause]

That is the end of Part Two.
Now turn to Part Three.

[pause]

PART 3   *You will hear an interview with an underwater photographer called Adam Pigot, who is talking about his work. For questions 15 to 20, choose the answer (A, B, C or D) which fits best according to what you hear.*

You now have one minute to look at Part Three.

[pause]

tone

Interviewer: My guest today is Adam Pigot, a commercial photographer who turned his back on conventional pictures and entered the more challenging world of underwater photography. Let's find out why. Adam, welcome.

Adam: Hello.

Interviewer: What tempted you to work underwater?

Adam: As a teenager, I became fascinated by film-making through my uncle, who was a famous film animator – I loved working in his studios. Then my life changed course when I joined the army and did adventure training, learning a range of skills from parachuting to skiing – but it was the sub-aqua diving which really struck a chord with me. I quickly tired of the military life and returned to the film world, getting a job as a cameraman on commercials. There I did a lot of photography, because I was always being asked to show pictures at production meetings. I took my camera with me everywhere, and the lure of diving made me try ways of taking photos underwater. I became a commercial photographer four years ago – I've never looked back!

Interviewer: Most of your work is in advertising – for sportswear manufacturers. Why?

Adam: The sportswear companies want to appeal to a young audience and as I used to be quite sporty, I'm on their wavelength. The previous adverts they'd done had been shot in the studio, using a team experienced in sports photography. But then the companies got new ideas and took me on to take bizarre shots, like people skiing underwater. I make the most of the unexpected when I'm working under the sea – huge fish could suddenly swim into the picture and I grab the chance to try out a new angle with my camera, to gain the best effects. There's not many of us do this type of photography, so I'm booked up well in advance, and you travel to some fantastic places – I certainly never get bored!

Interviewer: How do you choose your team?

Adam: You're only as good as the people you work with. Experience isn't everything underwater; the priority is keeping to an exact brief. So, I like to keep the team small – the model we're photographing, and one or two assistants in the water with me. Some of them are surprisingly young, but they're enthusiastic and open to new ideas, that's why I use them. The art director works from the boat – he likes to be involved at every stage. But he knows how important the choice of personnel is in marine photography, so he leaves that to me – after all, I'm the one who might need to be rescued!

Interviewer: So, you really have to trust your team.

Adam: Yes, it's important that the whole team observes the safety requirements – it's too easy to get lax. Before diving, we discuss the diving plan because there's little chance to communicate underwater. My reasoning is, we're not meant to be underwater in the first place, so the only way to remain safe is if everyone is aware that they're working in an alien environment, and knows exactly what they're doing. After all, it's often the 'happy accident' that makes a picture special, and you have to be ready to react to anything.

Interviewer:	You take some photos in the studio, don't you?
Adam:	Yes – in a deep water tank in the studio, which has advantages, as you avoid the huge cost of transporting all the equipment to some far-flung location. Though you never succeed in recreating some of the unique moments offered by nature when you're underwater in the sea. And the team can use a hydrophone – it's a kind of intercom, attached to a long cable, allowing those in the water to talk to those above. It gets annoying at times, keeping the cable out of the shot, but it saves people having to get out of the water because even at depths of two metres, you mustn't come up to the surface too rapidly.
Interviewer:	Using lights underwater must be difficult.
Adam:	I'm not a fan of artificial light, I only use it if I have to – if the cost can be justified. But you have to remember that water bends all lights, so it doesn't end up where you've directed it. And for the models it can be a bit off-putting. Most of my work involves looking up at the subject with the surface behind them – if a wave breaks when you press the shutter, you're never quite sure how a camera flash would react. Natural light is by far the best.
Interviewer:	So Adam, do you think this is a job for life?
Adam:	As long as I keep myself physically fit, there's no limit to what I can achieve underwater with all the technology that's now on offer.
Interviewer:	Thank you, Adam. And now ...

[pause]

Now you will hear Part Three again.

tone

[The recording is repeated.]

[pause]

That is the end of Part Three.
Now turn to Part Four.

[pause]

PART 4

Part Four consists of two tasks. You will hear five short extracts in which young people are talking about going shopping for clothes. Look at Task One. For questions 21 to 25, choose from the list (A to H) the reason each speaker gives for going clothes shopping. Now look at Task Two. For questions 26 to 30, choose from the list (A to H) the aspect of going clothes shopping that each speaker most enjoys. While you listen, you must complete both tasks.

You now have 45 seconds to look at Part Four.

[pause]

tone

Speaker One: I only buy clothes that are reduced – I can't afford them otherwise. I *love* shopping – it's my one chance to make up my own mind about things. I'm never sure what suits me, though. One day I'm going to have a personal dresser – you know, someone who rushes round finding outfits for you. My weight goes up and down like a yoyo, but I never throw clothes away, so if I've lost a few pounds, I just look in the wardrobe for last year's stuff. What *does* get me on the tram to the shops is when the sun comes out – I start thinking T-shirts, shorts and swimsuits!

[pause]

Speaker Two: None of my mates likes clothes shopping except Pete, so it's usually him who talks me into going with him. We both earn a good wage from our part-time jobs, so it's OK if we spend a lot. Sometimes we go for a haircut together – we always say we'll go for a different style but then we lose our nerve! I really like all the bustle and crowds in the city – it's just a shame we don't see more people we know. Anyway, sooner than you think, it's time to join the bus queue and go home, maybe empty-handed, maybe not.

[pause]

Speaker Three: I flick through magazines like *Cosmopolitan*, but I can't see myself in the clothes they photograph. Fashion's not important to me. If I'm going out somewhere with someone new, my friends all tell me to buy something special, but that just isn't me. Basically, I wear my favourite clothes till they fall apart, and then head off to the shops to find more of the same. It's not about looking for the cheapest option – in fact, I go for quality. One thing I really appreciate is a few quiet words with a good sales assistant – they know about fabrics, how to care for them and so on.

[pause]

Speaker Four: Sometimes I ask an assistant whether a jacket looks right on me, but I'm never sure they're being honest. Still, it's great seeing what's new in fashion. It makes you wonder if you should make some changes. I don't go clothes shopping as often as my friends. What I do is wait till I get a bonus from work, or get put on a better rate – then I go out and spend it! It's usually in winter, when it's cold here, but I buy clothes for all seasons, including boring things like socks while I'm at it. I'm a size larger now because I've put a few kilos on, but I look better like this.

[pause]

Speaker Five: It's all fun – bumping into people you know, having a coffee, looking at all the stuff in the shops – but nothing beats sitting on the bus, shopping bags around you, knowing you've got some great clothes. Back in your bedroom, you try it all on again and look forward to wearing it for real that night – I mean, that's the whole point of clothes shopping for me, you know, I go if I've got a party on or someone's asked me out. I might like the odd idea from one of the glossy magazines, but really I prefer starting from scratch and seeing what's available out there in the shops.

[pause]

Now you will hear Part Four again.

150

tone

[The recording is repeated.]

[pause]

That is the end of Part Four.

There will now be a pause of five minutes for you to copy your answers onto the separate answer sheet. Be sure to follow the numbering of all the questions. I shall remind you when there's one minute left, so that you're sure to finish in time.

[Teacher, pause the recording here for five minutes. Remind your students when they have one minute left.]

That is the end of the test. Please stop now. Your supervisor will now collect all the question papers and answer sheets.

Test 3 Key

Paper 1   Reading (1 hour 15 minutes)

Part 1

1 D   2 B   3 D   4 A   5 A   6 B

Part 2

7 B   8 D   9 G   10 A   11 E   12 F

Part 3

13 C   14 D   15 A   16 C   17 B   18 D   19 B

Part 4

20 B   21 D   22 A   23 C   24 D   25 B   26 C   27 D   28 C   29 A
30 C   31 D   32 A   33 D   34 B

Paper 2   Writing (1 hour 30 minutes)

Candidate responses are marked using the assessment scale on pages 122–123.

Paper 3   Use of English (1 hour)

Part 1

1 A   2 C   3 B   4 D   5 C   6 B   7 C   8 D   9 B   10 C
11 C   12 A

Part 2

13 according   14 to   15 us   16 more   17 order   18 with   19 them
20 out / off   21 such   22 this / it   23 after / upon   24 a / that   25 their
26 the   27 for

Part 3

28 publicity   29 atmospheric   30 significant   31 heroism   32 truly   33 competitive
34 likelihood   35 academics / academicians   36 courageous   37 unspoilt / unspoiled

Part 4

38 sharp   39 wing   40 roots   41 pressure   42 hit

Part 5

43 is / has (now) been | several decades SINCE   44 will have CROSSED | the desert in
45 WONDER if / whether | Ella (has / could have) left   46 resulted in / led to/meant / caused
| (a / some / the) LOSS of privacy   47 not / never have been | (put / left / placed) in CHARGE
48 a (good / high / great) / an impressive REPUTATION | for being / as OR the REPUTATION
| of being   49 been put FORWARD | to change / for changing   50 which | Clara TAKES after

Paper 4   Listening (approximately 40 minutes)

Part 1

1 A   **2** B   **3** A   **4** C   **5** C   **6** B

Part 2

7 (an / the) audio diary   **8** ecology   **9** fifteenth / 15th   **10** horse hair   **11** naturalist
12 mice   **13** (wooden) joints   **14** (water) pipes

Part 3

15 D   **16** A   **17** B   **18** D   **19** A   **20** C

Part 4

21 E   **22** D   **23** H   **24** C   **25** A   **26** F   **27** E   **28** C   **29** G   **30** B

Transcript	*This is the Cambridge Certificate in Advanced English Listening Test. Test Three.*
	I am going to give you the instructions for this test. I shall introduce each part of the test and give you time to look at the questions.
	At the start of each piece you will hear this sound:
	tone
	You will hear each piece twice.
	Remember, while you are listening, write your answers on the question paper. You will have five minutes at the end of the test to copy your answers onto the separate answer sheet.
	There will now be a pause. Please ask any questions now, because you must not speak during the test.
	[pause]
PART 1	*Now open your question paper and look at Part One.*
	[pause]
	You will hear three different extracts. For questions 1 to 6, choose the answer (A, B or C) which fits best according to what you hear. There are two questions for each extract.
Extract 1	*You hear part of a radio programme about an ancient factory in the south of Spain.*
	Now look at questions one and two.
	[pause]
	tone
Man:	Today in the History Programme Pippa Trevelyan is reporting from the ruins of an ancient Roman fish factory near Tarifa on the south coast of Spain.
Woman:	Well, this factory, where I'm standing now, used to produce huge quantities of a special spicy sauce that the Romans called 'garum'. The factory was a long

153

way outside the town, otherwise the inhabitants would've complained about the stench of rotten fish! Garum was a great favourite of the Romans' – it was shipped all over the empire and wealthy people paid the earth for it – they were the only ones who could afford it. You can easily get here on foot from the villages east or west of the ruins, taking the beach path. The bus is cheap, but only goes along the main road seven kilometres north of the site, so that's far from ideal. A convenient option is to drive in your own or a rented vehicle, but is that really as much fun as getting there under your own steam? I don't think so.

[pause]

tone

[The recording is repeated.]

[pause]

Extract 2

You hear a conversation between two inventors who have each made a lot of money.

Now look at questions three and four.

[pause]

tone

Man:	What's your definition of success?
Woman:	Success can be defined any number of ways. I personally have always defined it as waking every morning with a smile, looking forward to the day.
Man:	Or it's falling asleep at night dreaming about what adventure you might have next. For me, business isn't what I do for a living, it's a world where I can live out dreams and ideas. It's like taking part in a dangerous game, when the aim is to create a business that others thought was impossible.
Woman:	I enjoy risk, going against the grain of traditional business. When I come up with something unconventional, maybe a bit crazy, I get great pleasure from the critical looks of people who do things because they've always been done that way. It's their disbelief that gives me the energy to follow through on my vision.
Man:	I know what you mean. At the moment I'm investing in commercial spaceflight, which people say has to be my final venture. But it won't be. I'll hear about something that everyone else thinks is outrageous and do my best to make it a reality.

[pause]

tone

[The recording is repeated.]

[pause]

Extract 3	*You hear two students discussing a talk they have been to about mushrooms and other fungi.*
	Now look at questions five and six.
	[pause]
	tone
Man:	I thought that talk we had from one of the researchers on the project on mushrooms, sorry should use the correct word, fungi, was amazing!
Woman:	I know. I'd never even heard of this *Forgotten Kingdom* project. If I understood him right, there are pockets of experts doing different things, like making sure that all the species of fungus are documented in one area – and another team's looking at the effects of pollution on fungi – but what this project is doing is bringing all this expertise, their databases and so on, under one roof.
Man:	And that's what matters in work like this. People have to pool their knowledge. It seems to me though that what they're up against is apathy among ordinary people. Whether you've got two or twenty experts working on it, they'll need to be able to get funding for the management of more woodland and so on. If you haven't got the man in the street asking questions of the developers or asking awkward questions of their politicians, well it's a non-starter.
	[pause]
	tone
	[The recording is repeated.]
	[pause]
	That is the end of Part One. *Now turn to Part Two.*
	[pause]

PART 2	*You will hear a woman called Emma Karlsson introducing a programme about a very old house she has visited in the countryside. For questions 7 to 14, complete the sentences.*
	You now have 45 seconds to look at Part Two.
	[pause]
	tone
Emma:	Hello, and welcome to the programme. Today I want to introduce you to an old and very special house that I know, set deep in the heart of the countryside. In fact, the remainder of this programme will be less like my usual documentary and more of what you might call an audio diary about the old house as it rides through the seasons of the year, like a great ship at sea. I promise you, it's a feast for the ears which is not to be missed.

So, what's in the programme? I will be talking later to the current inhabitants of the house, who'll be giving me some insights into its present-day conservation. But my main focus will be on the building's ecology rather than its history or architectural significance. Indeed, this house has a life all of its own. Although the most recent parts only date back to the eighteenth century, much of the building was first put up in the fifteenth. And there is evidence that a building of some kind has occupied this site since the twelfth century. And, of course, all of this adds to its very special character.

Now, the building itself – the house was constructed using local materials as far as possible. For example, people think the straw used to make the roof came from the nearby fields. As for the walls, the builder used horse hair, which he mixed with plaster to make it stronger. He would have sourced these materials from the village. So you can't get much more local than that, can you?

So who lives here? Well, the house belongs to Roger Matthews, who as you might expect is now a naturalist, but he has also worked as a journalist and painter in his time. He shares the house with any number of creatures that come to find shelter or a place to rest – swallows and butterflies to name but a few. And some animal families must have lived here a long time. In particular, mice which have probably been in residence since the house was first built and can probably trace back their family line to their ancestors that first settled here when the foundations were laid.

Of course, apart from recordings about the house's many inhabitants, we've got all the natural noises from the house itself. For example, whenever the weather changes, the wooden joints all creak and groan so loudly that you can almost imagine them straining to take the weight of the house where the parts of its frame are fitted together. And thanks to the use of sophisticated recording techniques, there's a performance by a very special 'orchestra' – not a real one, of course, but rather all the water pipes in the house. The sounds these make are quite magical, even though some of them haven't actually performed their original function for many years. So, sit back and enjoy it all …

[pause]

tone

Now you will hear Part Two again.

[The recording is repeated.]

[pause]

That is the end of Part Two.
Now turn to Part Three.

[pause]

PART 3

You will hear part of an interview in which a jazz musician and radio presenter called Harry Bulford, is talking about his life and work. For questions 15 to 20, choose the answer (A, B, C or D) which fits best according to what you hear.

You now have one minute to look at Part Three.

[pause]

tone

Interviewer:	I'd like to welcome the radio presenter and musician Harry Bulford onto the programme. Harry, as our listeners will be aware, you're a first-class jazz player. What got you started initially?
Harry:	I always loved the rhythm of music, even when I was a little kid. Then I switched on the box one day and caught a glimpse of the great jazz musician Louis Armstrong lifting his trumpet to the sky, so I had a go at it myself and found I did have a sort of natural gift. Then I joined a band my brother set up – he was very keen on arranging gigs and so on. I didn't tap into the wistfulness, the heart-wrenching sadness of jazz at that point though, that came later on.
Interviewer:	Now, when you left school, you decided to attend music college. Why was that?
Harry:	My father hoped I'd become a teacher like him, but that was hardly in the scheme of things. I had this kind of idea I'd be able to earn a living writing concertos and symphonies for an admiring public, so I needed the training. That idea didn't work out, needless to say. But meanwhile I carried on doing solo gigs or sessions with the band, to keep my hand in. I remember that as students we liked being considered unconventional, a bit extreme even, but we were still part of the system and all needed to earn money.
Interviewer:	You've really built up your career as a jazz musician, so much so that several critics have given you the title of 'Britain's top trumpeter'. What's your reaction to that?
Harry:	Reviewers are fickle creatures. I could name at least five other musicians who've been called that in the last five years. I'm not ashamed to say that I know I'm good, and it's hardly a big deal being told so. What's important is to keep plugging away, extending, innovating all the time. It's a backhanded compliment anyway. It's implying nobody anywhere else has heard of you, which would be a pity if it were true.
Interviewer:	You're often on tour, giving performances all over the place. Has your appetite for this diminished in any way?
Harry:	Not at all. It's what I do. The thing is, I wake up every morning with my head full of tunes to try with the lads in the band. We've *almost* got used to each other's foibles – we're not there yet though! People say, 'You must enjoy getting feedback from fans,' well, not much chance of that, they're kept well away by the security people. It's a hectic few months, though, which does stretch you mentally and physically.
Interviewer:	So, how do you feel about leading a performer's life?
Harry:	It's been a huge amount of fun. I've never really experienced the financial ups and downs that others complain of. And I've made some great friends, though not from all walks of life, pretty much confined to the musical world. Hazard of the job, I suppose. You are away on tour a lot, and you have to make sure you spend quality time with your kids – luckily I've been able to do that. Another thing is that I've managed to keep out of the media spotlight, so they and my wife haven't suffered the way some families do.
Interviewer:	These days you're the presenter on a world music programme which has a devoted following. How did that come about?

| Harry: | Well, I was already presenting a jazz programme, but hardly anyone had heard of me then. I knew one of the producers quite well socially. I think he liked my no-nonsense style when presenting – I don't go in for flattery! So, he threw my name into the hat and I was asked to do a pilot programme. I had the time and I said yes. |
| Interviewer: | And it was an immediate hit. So, Harry, what plans do you have for … |

[pause]

tone

Now you will hear Part Three again.

[The recording is repeated.]

[pause]

That is the end of Part Three.
Now turn to Part Four.

[pause]

PART 4

Part Four consists of two tasks. You'll hear five short extracts in which people are talking about major changes in their lives. Look at Task One. For questions 21 to 25, choose from the list (A to H) each speaker's main reason for changing their life. Now look at Task Two. For questions 26 to 30, choose from the list (A to H) the feeling each speaker has about their new way of life. While you listen, you must complete both tasks.

You now have 45 seconds to look at Part Four.

[pause]

tone

| Speaker One: | I'd always liked the idea of flying, but when I was younger I was a music teacher, because the hours fitted in with my two sons. As they grew up, they became involved in aviation, so the conversation often revolved around planes. Then at fifty-two, after taking early retirement, I realised a lifetime's ambition and learned to fly – I loved it immediately! I completed my first long flight last year, circumnavigating the globe – I got sponsors and raised a lot of money for charity. It wasn't just completing the trip that gave me a big sense of achievement, it was helping people who are less fortunate. I've never done anything like that before. |

[pause]

| Speaker Two: | I'd been working in a bank for five years, and I thought, 'Do I want to do this forever?' I went on holiday and loved it – it was so different. I got to know the manager of the hotel where I was staying, they were very short-staffed and he gave me the chance to work in the office straightaway. I'd just got promotion at the bank, but, when a job like that lands in your lap, you can't pass it up. |

Life's very relaxed here, though you're not outside in the sun all day, like you are on holiday. But I couldn't imagine going back to nine to five every day and endless commuting. The salary isn't everything!

[pause]

Speaker Three: My father wanted me to become a lawyer, but left to my own devices I'd have done something more creative. Looking back, I found practising law very uncreative – and doing a job you dislike is soul-destroying. When the children's nanny left at short notice, it spurred me on to give up my job. I didn't want the children brought up by a series of strangers. So, I started going to art classes and painting at home – something I'd always wanted to do as a kid. Whenever I paint, it's so peaceful; I'm more laid-back now and I have a lot more time for people. I can do without the high income – my family comes first.

[pause]

Speaker Four: I was manager of a London department store, being nice to people all day and living for the hours when I could escape to ride my horse. I'd always loved horse-riding – I could practically ride before I could walk – but there I was slogging away working all hours to pay for a horse I barely had time to ride. I dreamed of running my own stable-yard. My friends said I was mad, but I gave up a secure job and put every penny into these run-down stables. Terrifying! But now I'm surrounded by fresh air and horses every day rather than cars and crowds. I drop into bed exhausted every night, but I feel so much better in myself.

[pause]

Speaker Five: I was working as a photographer. Then, while on holiday abroad, I saw this wonderful dancing! I started dancing classes as soon as I got home. At first it was just a hobby, but then I realised I was good enough to dance professionally – but that meant moving abroad. So, I left my friends and flew off to a new life! It was pretty scary – I had to succeed as a foreigner, and adapt to a different culture. But I walked straight off the plane into a job, and I haven't looked back since. I'm not a top star, but in the dance-world here everyone knows my name which counts for a lot – because it's a very competitive environment.

[pause]

tone

Now you will hear Part Four again.

[The recording is repeated.]

[pause]

That is the end of Part Four.

There will now be a pause of five minutes for you to copy your answers onto the separate answer sheet. Be sure to follow the numbering of all the questions. I shall remind you when there's one minute left, so that you're sure to finish in time.

[Teacher, pause the recording here for five minutes. Remind your students when they have one minute left.]

That is the end of the test. Please stop now. Your supervisor will now collect all the question papers and answer sheets.

Test 4 Key

Paper 1   Reading (1 hour 15 minutes)

Part 1

1 B   2 C   3 B   4 C   5 D   6 A

Part 2

7 B   8 G   9 D   10 A   11 E   12 F

Part 3

13 B   14 C   15 D   16 B   17 D   18 C   19 A

Part 4

20 C   21 A   22 C   23 B   24 C   25 A   26 D   27 B   28 A   29 D
30 B   31 D   32 C   33 D   34 B

Paper 2   Writing (1 hour 30 minutes)

Candidate responses are marked using the assessment scale on pages 122–123.

Paper 3   Use of English (1 hour)

Part 1

1 A   2 C   3 B   4 C   5 D   6 A   7 B   8 D   9 B   10 C
11 B   12 B

Part 2

13 was / is   14 their   15 what   16 it   17 another / others   18 at
19 having   20 of / about   21 after   22 to   23 for   24 someone / body /
anyone / body   25 this / that   26 in   27 as

Part 3

28 muddy   29 forested   30 literally   31 inhabitants   32 relocate
33 peacefully / peaceably   34 nearby   35 surrounding   36 necklaces   37 relatively

Part 4

38 ring   39 heart   40 soft   41 lives   42 played

Part 5

43 did not see | Mark (again) UNTIL   44 we do / finish our / the homework | before
GOING   45 PREVENT them | (from) being / getting OR PREVENT their / them | being /
getting   46 nothing (that / which) Jim | would NOT do   47 to have CHANGED | his mind
about   48 of closing | by the TIME (that)   49 (even) one / a single student / one of the
students | TURNED up   50 few GAPS | in Ann's knowledge

Paper 4   Listening (approximately 40 minutes)

Part 1

1 B   2 C   3 C   4 C   5 A   6 B

Part 2

7 ice skating   8 blue horizon   9 wetsuit   10 flags   11 anatomy   12 knees
13 (the) turns   14 flexibility

Part 3

15 C   16 B   17 D   18 A   19 D   20 B

Part 4

21 G   22 C   23 D   24 B   25 A   26 B   27 E   28 H   29 F   30 C

Transcript *This is the Cambridge Certificate in Advanced English Listening Test. Test Four.*

I am going to give you the instructions for this test. I shall introduce each part of the test and give you time to look at the questions.

At the start of each piece you will hear this sound:

tone

You will hear each piece twice.

Remember, while you are listening, write your answers on the question paper. You will have five minutes at the end of the test to copy your answers onto the separate answer sheet.

There will now be a pause. Please ask any questions now, because you must not speak during the test.

[pause]

PART 1   *Now open your question paper and look at Part One.*

[pause]

You will hear three different extracts. For questions 1 to 6, choose the answer (A, B or C) which fits best according to what you hear. There are two questions for each extract.

Extract 1   *You hear two students discussing projects they have to do in the final year of their course.*

Now look at questions one and two.

[pause]

tone

Woman: I'm impressed with your plan for your final year project. I haven't made my mind up what to do yet.

Man: You should do something with music. You've got the talent. I'm not sure I've got all the skills you need for my project.

Woman: You can't give up now. Just don't go for anything too ambitious.

Man: You're right. Anyway, I've got the idea for the story – it's science fiction, about human beings colonising another universe.

Woman: Very visual, not much talking.

Man: There's some good software for animation. It's expensive, but I think I'll get it.

Woman: It takes forever to learn how to use new computer stuff – at least it does me. We haven't got that long, remember. Just to the end of term.

Man: The software isn't a problem. It's putting everything together, so the story flows, so it's clear what's going on and there's no boring bits.

Woman: Yeah, that's important.

Man: Maybe you could do the music for it. I haven't a clue about that.

Woman: Would that be allowed, do you think? Put our projects together. It would be a lot of fun.

[pause]

tone

[The recording is repeated.]

[pause]

Extract 2   *You overhear a man telling a friend about an encounter with a bear during a recent trip to North America.*

Now look at questions three and four.

[pause]

tone

Woman: So, what's this I've heard about you and a bear?

Man: Oh … well, I've just been travelling across the States, and one day we'd camped in a dry river bed with a road bridge across it. Suddenly, I looked up and saw a bear ambling across the bridge. Unfortunately a car came along, the bear got scared and clambered over the side of the bridge where he got stuck on a narrow ledge.

Woman: Oh no! Don't tell me any more!

Man: Hmmmm … well, it had a happy ending – the bear was rescued, I promise – I was there to witness it. It was amazing! I called a rescue team.

Woman: For a *bear*?

Man: Why not? So they rushed out, tranquilised the bear, and lowered him down to the ground in a net. The bridge wasn't very high.

Woman: Poor old bear. He wasn't to know about cars and things … it's his habitat, after all. He was there first – they shouldn't invade his territory.

Man: Oh, the bear was completely unscathed – once he was on the ground he just wandered off as though nothing had happened.

Woman: Not very dignified for him, though … I wish I'd been there – you never know, I might've been able to help out …

Man: Mmm … well, at least he wasn't hurt …

[pause]

tone

[The recording is repeated.]

[pause]

Extract 3   *You overhear two friends talking about buying books.*

Now look at questions five and six.

[pause]

tone

Woman:	I've just been to the bookshop and bought a novel that looks great.
Man:	Don't you order books online? It's so convenient, you can do it any time.
Woman:	That's really handy, but you can't pick up the books and look at them, can you?
Man:	Hardly! But you can read reviews if you want on the website.
Woman:	That's true and they're well written on the whole. When I go into this shop, though, the staff ask a few questions and then point out something I wouldn't have thought of picking up, but which usually proves to be fascinating.
Man:	I'm always wary of doing that.
Woman:	Well, the other advantage of this place is they've just opened a café in a corner of the shop. I thought that was a bit pointless and they'd do better to use it for more bookshelves. As I sat there though, I realised you flick through and get the feel of a book before you commit yourself and you can chat in comfort with other customers who are probably people you've got something in common with – books!

[pause]

tone

[The recording is repeated.]

[pause]

That is the end of Part One.
Now turn to Part Two.

[pause]

PART 2   *You will hear a student called Guy Briggs giving a presentation at college about his experience of learning to surf. For questions 7 to 14, complete the sentences.*

You now have 45 seconds to look at Part Two.

[pause]

tone

Guy:	Hi everyone. My name's Guy Briggs, and I'd like to talk about what happened when I learnt to surf. Firstly, I should explain that before I tried surfing I'd dabbled in lots of other sports – I was a keen skier, did lots of cycle racing, and was obsessed with ice-skating and it was this sport which prepared me best for surfing, which I guess calls for some of the same skills.

Now, some people are self-taught surfers, but I wanted some tuition, so I went to a local school on Beach Parade which I'd certainly recommend. Unfortunately, it's rather inappropriately named *Blue Horizon* – when in fact the sea's always grey there. The waves aren't exactly enormous either, but the instructors were fantastic!

On day one, I was keen to get into my surfing gear and start looking the part. I'd invested in a smart pair of Hawaiian board shorts – so I was disappointed to find I looked awful in the wetsuit I was told to wear instead. However, my instructor insisted the key thing initially was safety, rather than appearance – although I think he was impressed with the waterproof watch I'd got myself. Anyway, he was right. Obviously if you don't know what to look out for in the water, you're risking trouble. You know, it's easy to be dragged out to sea by things like currents, so our instructor told us about flags that warn you about these, and which have to be observed. If they put one up on the beach when you're out surfing, you have to come back in. He also showed us where there were rocks out in the sea, and those areas were off-limits for both bathers and surfers at all times.

Then the instructor taught us all about the board itself – the shape, feel and weight of it, what he called its anatomy. I got the hang of carrying it, and how to 'pop up' onto it in five easy steps. This seemed straightforward on the beach, but more difficult out in the waves! It was great to actually get out onto the water, however.

On day two, we were reminded to do warm-up exercises before we started surfing, even though we still ached from the day before! This seemed a good idea, because I'd experienced some discomfort in my knees overnight, which I didn't want to make worse. In fact, however, the second day was less tiring and I even managed to surf in to the beach.

On the fourth day I made a breakthrough in the new moves I was learning – I was able to add 'turns' to the 'runs' I'd already mastered. These saved me from having to jump off the board when I started going too far out to sea! They're difficult, but once you manage them, you get a real thrill.

On the last day, we had a different instructor. Up till then, we'd heard all about stability, finding your centre of gravity, standing straight and looking cool. But this new bloke wanted to stress flexibility instead, saying *that* was the key – that way you're less likely to hurt yourself, like pulling a muscle, and the more competent a surfer you'll be.

So, all in all ...

[pause]

Now you will hear Part Two again.

tone

[The recording is repeated.]

[pause]

That is the end of Part Two.
Now turn to Part Three.

[pause]

PART 3

You will hear an interview with a singer-songwriter called Madeleine Marten, who is talking about her life and career. For questions 15 to 20, choose the answer (A, B, C or D) which fits best according to what you hear.

You now have one minute to look at Part Three.

[pause]

tone

Interviewer: I'm here today with singer-songwriter Madeleine Marten, who's been in the music business for thirty years! Welcome, Madeleine. Your early solo albums have just been re-released together with your first hit single, the one you made with the girl band *The Diamonds* almost thirty years ago.

Madeleine: That's right ...

Interviewer: And yet we still hear that single being played on the radio. Why has it lasted so well, do you think?

Madeleine: Well, *I'll* certainly always remember it, as the promotional video had the lowest ever budget! But strangely, we weren't even sure anyone would like it when it was first released, as the music seemed so experimental. Of course since then, some of the girls from the band have become household names in the world of pop. But I don't think any of those factors can account for its enduring popularity. The lyrics summed up important values and feelings that people still recognise today. I think that makes it sound very modern, somehow.

Interviewer: And the recording company encouraged you to change your name to Madeleine Marten – very different from your real name. How did that feel?

Madeleine: Well, once I'd been given the name, I immediately started thinking of myself as Madeleine. It did pose an identity problem back where I come from, though – a small down-to-earth-town – as no-one locally would call me by my professional name! Anyway, over the years I've gradually become both identities in most people's minds and the two have somehow merged now.

Interviewer: And recently you've also been appearing in a successful musical. What was that experience like?

Madeleine: Well, the offer of the part came along at just the right time. It got me back into the self-discipline of performing as a singer every night, and practising by day. I met great people, some of whom went on to appear on TV. But then after four years, I felt I'd gone as far as I could. Musicals aren't really my thing – I prefer watching stage plays, to be honest – and I felt I needed to get back to doing what I do best, which is writing songs.

Interviewer: And I believe one of the stars of the musical hit the newspaper headlines with reports about his behaviour during rehearsals.

Madeleine: Well, there really was nothing to report, but I think the public's obsessed with reading these stories. When people in show business behave badly, it's immediately in all the newspapers, whereas it would go unreported in other professions. Of course, truly awful behaviour is never acceptable, but it's important to distinguish between that, and someone whose apparent behaviour is actually part of their creative process. I think it's rarely due to a desire for publicity.

Interviewer:	And looking back over your career, are you satisfied with how it's turned out?
Madeleine:	Well, I've never really become that well known. Obviously you don't have much control over your work initially. You tend to take your manager's advice – and mine *was* good. But at one stage I was the backing singer for a really big and talented star, who had *total* control over her own work – but she clearly got that by being *very* assertive and explosive. I realised then that if that's what it took, then I didn't have the right temperament to become a big star. I'm more internal – I tend to think it's my fault when something doesn't go well, even though I'm sure of my talent. I don't know how healthy that is – but anyway, I'm happy with what I've achieved.
Interviewer:	But you've also written some new songs, haven't you? Tell us about those.
Madeleine:	Well, on some I've collaborated with a producer who's worked with some great singers. But I think now my work's slowly moving in a new direction, away from the pop career I had and more into world music. It's certainly more expressive of who I really am, and inevitably the lyrics are more mature now than they were when I was younger.
Interviewer:	Thanks, Madeleine.

[pause]

Now you will hear Part Three again.

tone

[The recording is repeated.]

[pause]

That is the end of Part Three.
Now turn to Part Four.

[pause]

PART 4

Part Four consists of two tasks. You will hear five short extracts in which people are talking about a change they are making in their lifestyles. Look at Task One. For questions 21 to 25, choose from the list (A to H) the lifestyle change each speaker is talking about. Now look at Task Two. For questions 26 to 30, choose from the list (A to H) each speaker's current feeling about their lifestyle change. While you listen you must complete both tasks.

You now have 45 seconds to look at Part Four.

[pause]

tone

Speaker One: The kids have been no help at all, but what's new? I was shocked to see just how much junk we as a family used to throw away every week – ten big bin bags! I thought, 'How am I going to cut that down to size?' But now I'm digging the vegetable peelings into the garden, and taking the empties to the bottle bank, on foot, I should add – that's probably keeping me pretty fit! The digging could do wonders for my waistline, but I don't know how long I can keep it up, I must say. It's rather a strain, and of course you have to remember to do it.

[pause]

Speaker Two: Who knows where we'll be in a few years' time? We might even make some serious money. In just three weeks – amazing, isn't it? – we've managed to get it together and even think of a name! We had our first rehearsal last week – it was quite energetic, and I really enjoyed myself. The next thing is to set up some gigs – they'll have to be at weekends, because we've all got full-time jobs and no plans to branch out from that. I got my licence a couple of years back so I'll probably be the driver as well! But the other guys will be contributing in other ways, I'm sure.

[pause]

Speaker Three: For the last three weekends I've been out with the countryside rangers, helping to clear footpaths and pick up rubbish. They need people to devote a bit of their spare time to it – there just aren't the funds available to pay for this sort of thing. At the end of each day I was physically exhausted, ate a huge meal, and went out like a light. Of course, I've had to give up my Saturday job at the garage, which means I'll be broke by the end of the month – not that that'll stop me. I could ask my family for a loan. They've always supported green issues; I'm just hoping they'll be able to help me out.

[pause]

Speaker Four: My travel arrangements are still chaotic, especially in the mornings, because bus and train times don't co-ordinate well on my daily commute, and I always have to run to catch the early bus. Luckily my boss is very understanding if I turn up late, and hardly ever tells me off! I've had some lessons already, and I hope to take my test early next year, so that'll help, especially when it comes to getting around on my own. It's a painfully slow process though, and I'm still finding it really hard. My instructor feels I could do better, and I'm sure he's right. I know I'll get there in the end though.

[pause]

Speaker Five: Now I've enrolled on this computer course, I feel a lot better about my day job. The boss doesn't appreciate that I want something more out of life than packing biscuits forever, you know? He's really infuriating – he thinks that's all I can do! I told him straight, 'I'll be leaving this place much sooner than you think.' The other girls all clapped. Well, that'll teach him. The course is really tough and we get homework and everything. So there's no time for me to do all my usual things like keeping up with my favourite bands or going running. I think I can handle it though.

[pause]

Now you will hear Part Four again.

tone

[The recording is repeated.]

[pause]

That is the end of Part Four.

There will now be a pause of five minutes for you to copy your answers onto the separate answer sheet. Be sure to follow the numbering of all the questions. I'll remind you when there's one minute left, so that you are sure to finish in time.

[Teacher, pause the recording here for five minutes. Remind your students when they have one minute left.]

That is the end of the test. Please stop now. Your supervisor will now collect all the question papers and answer sheets.

UNIVERSITY *of* CAMBRIDGE
ESOL Examinations

Candidate Name
If not already printed, write name
in CAPITALS and complete the
Candidate No. grid (in pencil).

Candidate Signature

Examination Title

Centre

Supervisor:
If the candidate is ABSENT or has WITHDRAWN shade here ▭

Centre No.

Candidate No.

**Examination
Details**

Candidate Answer Sheet

Instructions

Use a PENCIL (B or HB).

Mark ONE letter for each question.

For example, if you think B is the right answer to the question, mark your answer sheet like this:

Rub out any answer you wish to change using an eraser.

1	A B C D E F G H
2	A B C D E F G H
3	A B C D E F G H
4	A B C D E F G H
5	A B C D E F G H
6	A B C D E F G H
7	A B C D E F G H
8	A B C D E F G H
9	A B C D E F G H
10	A B C D E F G H
11	A B C D E F G H
12	A B C D E F G H
13	A B C D E F G H
14	A B C D E F G H
15	A B C D E F G H
16	A B C D E F G H
17	A B C D E F G H
18	A B C D E F G H
19	A B C D E F G H
20	A B C D E F G H

21	A B C D E F G H
22	A B C D E F G H
23	A B C D E F G H
24	A B C D E F G H
25	A B C D E F G H
26	A B C D E F G H
27	A B C D E F G H
28	A B C D E F G H
29	A B C D E F G H
30	A B C D E F G H
31	A B C D E F G H
32	A B C D E F G H
33	A B C D E F G H
34	A B C D E F G H
35	A B C D E F G H
36	A B C D E F G H
37	A B C D E F G H
38	A B C D E F G H
39	A B C D E F G H
40	A B C D E F G H

A-H 40 CAS

denote Print Limited 0121 520 5100

DP594/300

Sample answer sheet: Paper 3

UNIVERSITY of CAMBRIDGE
ESOL Examinations

S A M P L E

Candidate Name
If not already printed, write name in CAPITALS and complete the Candidate No. grid (in pencil).

Candidate Signature

Examination Title

Centre

Supervisor:
If the candidate is ABSENT or has WITHDRAWN shade here

Centre No.

Candidate No.

Examination Details

0	0	0	0
1	1	1	1
2	2	2	2
3	3	3	3
4	4	4	4
5	5	5	5
6	6	6	6
7	7	7	7
8	8	8	8
9	9	9	9

Instructions
Use a PENCIL (B or HB).
Rub out any answer you wish to change.

Part 1: Mark ONE letter for each question.
For example, if you think B is the right answer to the question, mark your answer sheet like this:

0 A B̶ C D

Parts 2, 3, 4 and **5:** Write your answer clearly in CAPITAL LETTERS.

For Parts 2, 3 and 4, write one letter in each box.

0 E X A M P L E

Candidate Answer Sheet

Part 2

Do not write below here

Part 1				
1	A	B	C	D
2	A	B	C	D
3	A	B	C	D
4	A	B	C	D
5	A	B	C	D
6	A	B	C	D
7	A	B	C	D
8	A	B	C	D
9	A	B	C	D
10	A	B	C	D
11	A	B	C	D
12	A	B	C	D

13 13 1 0 u
14 14 1 0 u
15 15 1 0 u
16 16 1 0 u
17 17 1 0 u
18 18 1 0 u
19 19 1 0 u
20 20 1 0 u
21 21 1 0 u
22 22 1 0 u
23 23 1 0 u
24 24 1 0 u
25 25 1 0 u
26 26 1 0 u
27 27 1 0 u

Continues over ➡

CAE UoE

DP597/301

© UCLES 2012 Photocopiable

171

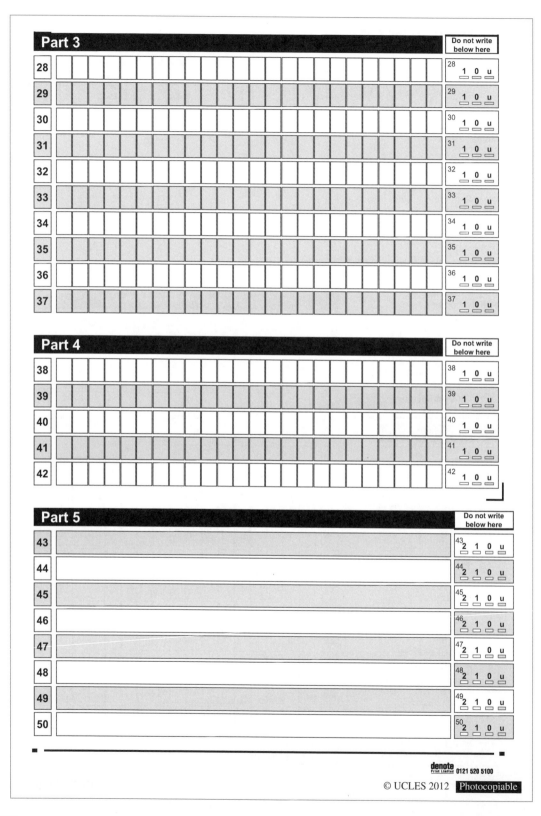

denote
Print Limited 0121 520 5100

Sample answer sheet: Paper 4

S A M P L E

Candidate Name
If not already printed, write name
in CAPITALS and complete the
Candidate No. grid (in pencil).

Candidate Signature

Examination Title

Centre

Supervisor:
If the candidate is ABSENT or has WITHDRAWN shade here ⬚

Centre No.

Candidate No.

**Examination
Details**

0	0	0	0
1	1	1	1
2	2	2	2
3	3	3	3
4	4	4	4
5	5	5	5
6	6	6	6
7	7	7	7
8	8	8	8
9	9	9	9

Test version: A B C D E F J K L M N   Special arrangements: S H

Candidate Answer Sheet

Instructions

Use a PENCIL (B or HB).
Rub out any answer you wish to change using an eraser.

Parts 1, 3 and **4:**
Mark ONE letter for each question.

For example, if you think **B** is the
right answer to the question, mark
your answer sheet like this:

Part 2:
Write your answer clearly in CAPITAL LETTERS.

Write one letter or number in each box.
If the answer has more than one word, leave one
box empty between words.

For example:

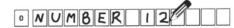

Turn this sheet over to start.

Part 1

	A	B	C
1	⊂⊃	⊂⊃	⊂⊃
2	⊂⊃	⊂⊃	⊂⊃
3	⊂⊃	⊂⊃	⊂⊃
4	⊂⊃	⊂⊃	⊂⊃
5	⊂⊃	⊂⊃	⊂⊃
6	⊂⊃	⊂⊃	⊂⊃

Part 2 (Remember to write in CAPITAL LETTERS or numbers)

Do not write below here

7		7 1 0 u
8		8 1 0 u
9		9 1 0 u
10		10 1 0 u
11		11 1 0 u
12		12 1 0 u
13		13 1 0 u
14		14 1 0 u

Part 3

	A	B	C	D
15	⊂⊃	⊂⊃	⊂⊃	⊂⊃
16	⊂⊃	⊂⊃	⊂⊃	⊂⊃
17	⊂⊃	⊂⊃	⊂⊃	⊂⊃
18	⊂⊃	⊂⊃	⊂⊃	⊂⊃
19	⊂⊃	⊂⊃	⊂⊃	⊂⊃
20	⊂⊃	⊂⊃	⊂⊃	⊂⊃

Part 4

	A	B	C	D	E	F	G	H
21	⊂⊃	⊂⊃	⊂⊃	⊂⊃	⊂⊃	⊂⊃	⊂⊃	⊂⊃
22	⊂⊃	⊂⊃	⊂⊃	⊂⊃	⊂⊃	⊂⊃	⊂⊃	⊂⊃
23	⊂⊃	⊂⊃	⊂⊃	⊂⊃	⊂⊃	⊂⊃	⊂⊃	⊂⊃
24	⊂⊃	⊂⊃	⊂⊃	⊂⊃	⊂⊃	⊂⊃	⊂⊃	⊂⊃
25	⊂⊃	⊂⊃	⊂⊃	⊂⊃	⊂⊃	⊂⊃	⊂⊃	⊂⊃
26	⊂⊃	⊂⊃	⊂⊃	⊂⊃	⊂⊃	⊂⊃	⊂⊃	⊂⊃
27	⊂⊃	⊂⊃	⊂⊃	⊂⊃	⊂⊃	⊂⊃	⊂⊃	⊂⊃
28	⊂⊃	⊂⊃	⊂⊃	⊂⊃	⊂⊃	⊂⊃	⊂⊃	⊂⊃
29	⊂⊃	⊂⊃	⊂⊃	⊂⊃	⊂⊃	⊂⊃	⊂⊃	⊂⊃
30	⊂⊃	⊂⊃	⊂⊃	⊂⊃	⊂⊃	⊂⊃	⊂⊃	⊂⊃

Thanks and acknowledgements

The authors and publishers acknowledge the following sources of copyright material and are grateful for the permissions granted. While every effort has been made, it has not always been possible to identify the sources of all the material used, or to trace all copyright holders. If any omissions are brought to our notice, we will be happy to include the appropriate acknowledgements on reprinting.

Icon Magazine for the text on p. 8 adapted from 'What is design' by Marcus Fairs, *Icon Magazine* December 2004. Reproduced with permission; NI Syndication Limited for the text on p. 9 adapted from 'Roadtrip Nation: Dr Andrew Steele' *The Times* 16.11.06, for the text on p. 34 adapted from 'Look back in anger' by Sheila Keating, *The Times Magazine* 20.10.02, for the text on p. 35 adapted from 'The Feelgood Factor' by Dr Nick Bayliss, *The Times Magazine* 06.09.03, for the text on p. 38 adapted from 'Life is beautiful without a camera' by Rupert Watson, *The Times* 07.10.00, for the text on p. 93 adapted from 'Special supplement: Engineering in Sport' by Tim Clifford, *The Sunday Times* 04.07.04. Copyright © NI Syndication Limited; Telegraph Media Group Limited for the text on pp. 10–11 adapted from 'Spadework that's truly rewarding' by Tony Durrant, *The Daily Telegraph* 14.04.01. Copyright © Telegraph Media Group Limited 2001; Word Magazine for the text on p. 12 adapted from 'And another thing' by David Hepworth, *Word Magazine* September 2007. Reproduced with permission; Chelsea Magazine Company Ltd for the text on p. 15 adapted from 'An Undying Art' by Laura Gascoigne, *Artists & Illustrators* May 2001. Reproduced with permission; text on p. 33 adapted from 'Human Behaviour' by Susan Aldridge, *Focus Magazine* June 2004; The Independent for the text on pp. 36–37 adapted from 'The future of writing' by Paul Roberts, *Independent on Sunday* 29.09.96. Copyright © The Independent 1996; Immediate Media Company Bristol Limited for the text on p. 41 adapted from 'Introduced Mammals of the World' by John Burton, original source *BBC Wildlife Magazine* July 2004, for the text on p. 41 adapted from 'The New Encyclopedia of Insects and their Allies' by Richard Jones, original source *BBC Wildlife Magazine* February 2003. Copyright © Immediate Media Company Bristol Limited; ThinkBuzan for the text on p. 59 adapted from www.thinkbuzan.com. Reproduced with permission; The Random House Group Limited and Random House Inc for the text on p. 61 adapted from *Engleby: A Novel* by Sebastian Faulks, copyright © 2007 by Sebastian Faulks. Published by Vintage Books. Used by permission of Doubleday, a division of Random House, Inc and The Random House Group Limited; William Morris Endeavor Entertainment, LLC for the text on p. 64 adapted from *A House Somewhere: Tales of Life Abroad.* Copyright © 2011 by Simon Winchester, published by Lonely Planet 2011; Text on p. 67 adapted from 'A new string to Maxim's bow' by Michael Church, *The Independent Friday Review* 11.06.99; The Random House Group Limited and The Nicholas Ellison Agency for the text on p. 85 adapted from *The Rule of Four* by Ian Caldwell and Dustin Thomason, published by Century. Reprinted by permission of The Random House Group Limited and The Nicholas Ellison Agency; text on p. 86 adapted from *The Centre of the Bed* by Joan Bakewell, 2003, published by Hodder & Stoughton; Susan Bergholz Literary Services for the text on pp. 88–89 adapted from *Heart and Blood, Living with Deer in America.* Copyright © 1997 by Richard Nelson. Published by Vintage Books and originally in hardcover by Alfred A. Knopf, Inc, a division of Random House, Inc, New York. By permission of Susan Bergholz Literary Services, New York, NY and Lamy, NM. All rights reserved; Guardian News and Media Ltd for the text on p. 90 adapted from 'Highly Evolved' by Simon Armitage, *The Observer* 12.07.09. Copyright © Guardian News & Media Ltd 2009.

Photo acknowledgements

The authors and publishers acknowledge the following sources of copyright material and are grateful for the permissions granted. While every effort has been made, it has not always been possible to identify the sources of all the material used, or to trace all copyright holders. If any omissions are brought to our notice, we will be happy to include the appropriate acknowledgements on reprinting.

p. 11: copyright Canterbury Archaeological Trust Ltd; p. 47: imagebroker.net/SuperStock; p. 54: Mike Rex/ Alamy; p. 89: Don Hooper/Alamy; p. C1 (TL): Pierre Tremblay/Masterfile; p. C1 (TR): Rene de Wit/Arcaid/ Corbis; p. C1 (B): Blend Images/SuperStock; p. C2 (T): Douglas O'Connor/Alamy; p. C2 (C): Yellow Dog Productions/Getty Images; p. C2 (B): David De Lossy/Thinkstock; p. C3 (TL): Creatas/Thinkstock; p. C3 (TR): Phil Date/iStockphoto; p. C3 (CL): Nicholas J Reid/Getty Images; p. C3 (C): Nic Bothma/epa/Corbis; p. C3 (CR): William Casey/Shutterstock; p. C3 (BL), C5 (T) and C9 (TC): Thinkstock; p. C3 (BR): Photofusion Picture Library/Alamy; p. C4 (T): Rich Legg/iStockphoto; p. C4 (C): Ian West/PA Wire/Press Association Images; p. C4 (B): Visual&Written SL/Alamy; p. C5 (C): Clay McLachlan/Getty Images; p. C5 (B): Szasz-Fabian Ilka Erika/Shutterstock; p. C6 (TL): parasola.net/Alamy; p. C6 (TR): Mike Booth/Alamy; p. C6 (CL): Fancy/Alamy; p. C6 (CR): Paul Rapson/Alamy; p. C6 (BL): Science Museum/Science & Society Picture Library all rights reserved; p. C6 (BR): AlamyCelebrity/Alamy; p. C7 (T): Jeremy Nicholl/Alamy; p. C7 (BL): David Robertson/Alamy; p. C7 (BR): Robert Convery/Alamy; p. C8 (TL): Charlotte Nation/Getty Images; p. C8 (TR): Gunter Marx/Alamy; p. C8 (B): imagebroker.net/SuperStock; p. C9 (TL): Anna Hoychuk/Shutterstock; p. C9 (TR): Pascal Broze/Getty Images; p. C9 (CL): Cecilia Cartner/cultura/Corbis; p. C9 (CR): Jupiterimages/ Thinkstock; p. C9 (BL): kuttig-RF-Kids/Alamy; p. C9 (BR): Lonely Planet Images/Alamy; p. C10 (T): Paul Souders/Corbis; p. C10 (C): Alex Treadway/National Geographic Society/Corbis; p. C10 (B): Frank Krahmer/ Corbis; p. C11 (T); Design Pics/SuperStock; p. C11 (C): Jeff Morgan 14/Alamy; p. C11 (B): Richard Levine/ Alamy; p. C12 (TL): Glow Images; p. C12 (TR): Monty Rakusen/cultura/Corbis; p. C12 (CL): David Cole/ Alamy; p. C12 (CR): Garry Gay/Getty Images; p. C12 (BL): Hank Morgan/Science Photo Library; p. C12 (BR): BananaStock/Thinkstock.

Design concept by Peter Ducker

The recordings which accompany this book were made at dsound, London.